RAIDS ON THE UNSPEAKABLE

By Thomas Merton

Published by
New Directions

Raids on the Unspeakable

Thomas Merton

NEW DIRECTIONS

Library of Congress Catalog Card Number: 66-17823 (ISBN: 0-8112-0101-5)

Manufactured in the United States of America. Published in Canada by McClelland & Stewart, Ltd.

New Directions books are published for James Laughlin by New Directions Publishing Corporation, 333 Sixth Avenue, New York 10014.

FIFTH PRINTING

Today the first and perhaps the only duty of the philosopher is to defend man against himself: to defend man against that extraordinary temptation toward inhumanity to which —almost without being aware of it—so many human beings today have yielded.

GABRIEL MARCEL

Contents

Prologue

WELL, *Raids*, you're grown up now. It is time for you to go out and meet people as the other books have done. They have usually managed pretty well on their own. They were, for the most part, good mannered. Some of them were even fairly devout. As for you, you may need special advice. I must say you have proved yourself to be a little unusual. It's your poetic temperament. I would hardly call you devout, though I have found you meditating in your own way (not often in Church). But you must remember that most of your brothers went to the seminary, and you will be expected to act like a seminarian yourself. This, I fear, is where you will run into trouble. Take your cosmological myths, for example. You must make clear somehow, particularly to the clergy, that your "Atlas" has a rather peculiar ontological status. He is not "God" by any means. He is a titan. There are no titans in the philosophy books, you know. You tell me he is "nature." You immediately qualify that by saying he is not "physical nature, but rather the natural creativity of the free subject as microcosm," or some such expression. Now this kind of thing is all right for someone like Berdyaev, but you are likely to get me into trouble. Will you be careful, please, not to overemphasize the titans, the creativity, and the microcosmic subject? And don't make Atlas look like a "world soul" or a cosmic Adam. I have been called so many names lately that I don't want to be called a gnostic anarchist on top of everything else. Please think of your old man, won't you?

Yet I must admit I would be disappointed if no one got your message. Because you do have a message, and I must say I rather like it myself. I feel that though you are definitely a bit wild, your intuitions hit a few targets that the other books may have missed. Mind you, I do not repudiate the other books. I love the whole lot of you. But in some ways, *Raids*, I think I love you more than the rest.

You are not so much concerned with ethical principles and traditional answers to traditional questions, for many men have decided no longer to ask themselves these questions. Your main interest is not in formal answers or accurate definitions, but in difficult insights at a moment of human crisis. Such insights can hardly be either comforting or well defined: they are obscure and ironic. They cannot be translated into a program for solving all the problems of society, but they may perhaps enable a rare person here and there to come alive and be awake at a moment when wakefulness is desirable—a moment of ultimate choice, in which he finds himself challenged in the roots of his own existence. You have considered the critical challenge of the hour, that of dehumanization, and have dealt with it as you could, with poetry and irony rather than tragic declamation or confessional formulas.

I have mentioned Berdyaev. You are certainly not as ambitious as he was, but you have something of the same eschatological temper. Do not imagine that this will win you every heart. Far from it! Remember that Berdyaev was thrown into prison twice by the tsars and then twice again by the Communists who finally exiled him. There are no more tsars, fortunately. But that does not mean that there is no absolutism in the world. Quite the contrary! There is now a bargain-absolutism for the many which has replaced the exclusive-absolutism of the few. Once you consent to let yourself be "levelled" in Kierkegaard's sense, you become a little tsar in a mass of tsars—you belong to the absolutism of the world of managers and military brass. In this all our social systems are alike, whether communist or capitalist.

You have derided this "tsardom" in your "Fat Man," and in the "Rhinoceros" (borrowed from Ionesco). You have spoken of it to poets and artists. In these and other symbols you express what you do not accept in the modern world: the *hubris* of affluence and power and the communion in arrogance which makes tsars out of mice.

Make no mistake; this is not a popular message. Such sentiments are acceptable only when they are concentrated in an attack upon *the other side*: "communist" or "imperialist," as the case may be. If you insist on disapproving of everybody, you will certainly have few friends. But of course, it is not persons you disapprove of: it is ideas. And you do have friends: the young poets, and the "new men," for instance, or else simply "people" as people, not as functionaries or commissars.

The Unspeakable. What is this? Surely, an eschatological image. It is the void that we encounter, you and I, underlying the announced programs, the good intentions, the unexampled and universal aspirations for the best of all possible worlds. It is the void that contradicts everything that is spoken even before the words are said; the void that gets into the language of public and official declarations at the very moment when they are pronounced, and makes them ring dead with the hollowness of the abyss. It is the void out of which Eichmann drew the punctilious exactitude of his obedience, the void which drawls in the zany violence of Flannery O'Connor's Southerners, or hypnotizes the tempted conscience in Julien Green. It is the emptiness of "the end." Not necessarily the end of the world, but a theological point of no return, a climax of absolute finality in refusal, in equivocation, in disorder, in absurdity, which can be broken open again to truth only by miracle, by the coming of God. Yet nowhere do you despair of this

4

miracle. You seem to say that, for you, this is precisely what it means to be a Christian; for Christian hope begins where every other hope stands frozen stiff before the face of the Unspeakable. I am glad you say this, but you will not find too many agreeing with you, even among Christians.

Returning once again to Berdyaev—perhaps you would concur with this statement of his (from *Dream and Reality*): "Eschatology is not an invitation to escape into a private heaven: it is a call to transfigure the evil and stricken world. It is a witness to the end of this world of ours with its enslaving objectifications . . ." Personally, I am not too sure that all "objectifications" are "enslaving" and I know your existentialism is not one of pure subjectivity. As to the world being "evil," that too needs to be qualified. Your "Atlas" is precisely the world *as good*. The goodness of the world, stricken or not, is incontestable and definitive. If it is stricken, it is also healed in Christ. But nevertheless one of the awful facts of our age is the evidence that it is stricken indeed, stricken to the very core of its being by the presence of the Unspeakable.

Those who are at present so eager to be reconciled with the world at any price must take care not to be reconciled with it under this particular aspect: *as the nest of the Unspeakable*. This is what too few are willing to see.

Well, we accept that particular statement of Berdyaev's only with reservations. How about this one: "The practical conclusion derived from this faith [eschatological Christianity] turns into an accusation of the age in which I live and into a command to be human in this most inhuman of ages, to guard the image of man for it is the image of God."

You are not big enough to accuse the whole age effectively, but let us say you are in dissent. You are in no position to issue commands, but you can speak words of hope. Shall this be the substance of your message? Be human in this most inhuman of ages; guard the image of man for it is the image of God. You agree? Good. Then go with my blessing. But I warn you, do not expect to make many friends. As for the Unspeakable—his implacable presence will not be disturbed by a little fellow like you!

Abbey of Gethsemani
Fall, 1965.

6

Rain and the Rhinoceros

LET me say this before rain becomes a utility that they can plan and distribute for money. By "they" I mean the people who cannot understand that rain is a festival, who do not appreciate its gratuity, who think that what has no price has no value, that what cannot be sold is not real, so that the only way to make something *actual* is to place it on the market. The time will come when they will sell you even your rain. At the moment it is still free, and I am in it. I celebrate its gratuity and its meaninglessness.

The rain I am in is not like the rain of cities. It fills the woods with an immense and confused sound. It covers the flat roof of the cabin and its porch with insistent and controlled rhythms. And I listen, because it reminds me again and again that the whole world runs by rhythms I have not yet learned to recognize, rhythms that are not those of the engineer.

I came up here from the monastery last night, sloshing through the cornfield, said Vespers, and put some oatmeal on the Coleman stove for supper. It boiled over while I was listening to the rain and toasting a piece of bread at the log fire. The night became very dark. The rain surrounded the whole cabin with its enormous virginal myth, a whole world of meaning, of secrecy, of silence, of rumor. Think of it: all that speech pouring down, selling nothing, judging nobody, drenching the thick mulch of dead leaves, soaking the trees, filling the gullies and crannies of the wood with water, washing out the places where men have stripped the hillside! What a thing it is to sit absolutely alone, in the forest, at night, cherished by this wonderful, unintelligible, perfectly innocent speech, the most comforting speech in the world, the talk that rain makes by itself all over the ridges, and the talk of the watercourses everywhere in the hollows!

Nobody started it, nobody is going to stop it. It will talk as long as it wants, this rain. As long as it talks I am going to listen.

But I am also going to sleep, because here in this wilderness I have learned how to sleep again. Here I am not alien. The trees I know, the night I know, the rain I know. I close my eyes and instantly sink into the whole rainy world of which I am a part, and the world goes on with me in it, for I am not alien to it. I am alien to the noises of cities, of people, to the greed of machinery that does not sleep, the hum of power that eats up the night. Where rain, sunlight and darkness are contemned, I cannot sleep. I do not trust anything that has been fabricated to replace the climate of woods or prairies. I can have no confidence in places where the air is first fouled and then cleansed, where the water is first made deadly and then made safe with other poisons. There is nothing in the world of buildings that is not fabricated, and if a tree gets in among the apartment houses by mistake it is taught to grow chemically. It is given a precise reason for existing. They put a sign on it saying it is for health, beauty, perspective; that it is for peace, for prosperity; that it was planted by the mayor's daughter. All of this is mystification. The city itself lives on its own myth. Instead of waking up and silently existing, the city people prefer a stubborn and fabricated dream; they do not care to be a part of the night, or to be merely of the world. They have constructed a world outside the world, against the world, a world of mechanical fictions which contemn nature and seek only to use it up, thus preventing it from renewing itself and man.

Of course the festival of rain cannot be stopped, even in the city. The woman from the delicatessen scampers along the sidewalk with a newspaper over her head. The streets, suddenly washed, became transparent and alive, and the noise of traffic becomes a plashing of fountains. One would think that urban man in a rainstorm would *have* to take account of nature in its wetness and freshness, its baptism and its renewal. But the rain brings no renewal to the city, only to tomorrow's weather, and the glint of windows in tall buildings will then have nothing to do with the new sky. All "reality" will remain somewhere inside those walls, counting itself and selling itself with fantastically complex determination. Meanwhile the obsessed citizens plunge through the rain bearing the load of their obsessions, slightly more vulnerable than before, but still only barely aware of external realities. They do not see that the streets shine beautifully, that they themselves are walking on stars and water, that they are running in skies to catch a bus or a taxi, to shelter somewhere in the press of irritated humans, the faces of advertisements and the dim, cretinous sound of unidentified music. But they must know that there is wetness abroad. Perhaps they even *feel* it. I cannot say. Their complaints are mechanical and without spirit.

Naturally no one can believe the things they say about the rain. It all implies one basic lie: *only the city is real.* That weather, not being planned, not being fabricated, is an impertinence, a wen on the visage of progress. (Just a simple little operation, and the whole mess may become relatively tolerable. Let business *make* the rain. This will give it meaning.)

THOREAU sat in *his* cabin and criticized the railways. I sit in mine and wonder about a world that has, well, progressed. I must read *Walden* again, and see if Thoreau already guessed that he was part of what he thought he could escape. But it is not a matter of "escaping." It

12

is not even a matter of protesting very audibly. Technology is here, even in the cabin. True, the utility line is not here yet, and so G.E. is not here yet either. When the utilities and G.E. enter my cabin arm in arm it will be nobody's fault but my own. I admit it. I am not kidding anybody, even myself. I will suffer their bluff and patronizing complacencies in silence. I will let them think they know what I am doing here.

They are convinced that *I am having fun.*

This has already been brought home to me with a wallop by my Coleman lantern. Beautiful lamp: It burns white gas and sings viciously but gives out a splendid green light in which I read Philoxenos, a sixth-century Syrian hermit. Philoxenos fits in with the rain and the festival of night. Of this, more later. Meanwhile: what does my Coleman lantern tell me? (Coleman's philosophy is printed on the cardboard box which I have (guiltily) not shellacked as I was supposed to, and which I have tossed in the woodshed behind the hickory chunks.) Coleman says that the light is good, and has a reason: it *"Stretches days to give more hours of fun."*

Can't I just be in the woods without any special reason? Just being in the woods, at night, in the cabin, is something too excellent to be justified or explained! It just *is*. There are always a few people who are in the woods at night, in the rain (because if there were not the world would have ended), and I am one of them. We are not having fun, we are not "having" anything,

13

we are not *"stretching our days,"* and if we had fun it would not be measured by hours. Though as a matter of fact that is what fun seems to be: a state of diffuse excitation that can be measured by the clock and "stretched" by an appliance.

There is no clock that can measure the speech of this rain that falls all night on the drowned and lonely forest.

Of course at three-thirty A.M. the SAC plane goes over, red light winking low under the clouds, skimming the wooded summits on the south side of the valley, loaded with strong medicine. Very strong. Strong enough to burn up all these woods and stretch our hours of fun into eternities.

AND that brings me to Philoxenos, a Syrian who had fun in the sixth century, without benefit of appliances, still less of nuclear deterrents.

Philoxenos in his ninth *memra* (on poverty) to dwellers in solitude, says that there is no explanation and no justification for the solitary life, since it is without a law. To be a contemplative is therefore to be an outlaw. As was Christ. As was Paul.

One who is not "alone," says Philoxenos, has not discovered his identity. He seems to be alone, perhaps, for he experiences himself as "individual." But because he is willingly enclosed and limited by the laws and illusions of collective existence, he has no more identity

14

than an unborn child in the womb. He is not yet conscious. He is alien to his own truth. He has senses, but he cannot use them. He has life, but no identity. To have an identity, he has to be awake, and aware. But to be awake, he has to accept vulnerability and death. Not for their own sake: not out of stoicism or despair—only for the sake of the invulnerable inner reality which we cannot recognize (which we can only *be*) but to which we awaken only when we see the unreality of our vulnerable shell. The discovery of this inner self is an act and affirmation of solitude.

Now if we take our vulnerable shell to be our true identity, if we think our mask is our true face, we will protect it with fabrications even at the cost of violating our own truth. This seems to be the collective endeavor of society: the more busily men dedicate themselves to it, the more certainly it becomes a collective illusion, until in the end we have the enormous, obsessive, uncontrollable dynamic of fabrications designed to protect mere fictitious identities—"selves," that is to say, regarded as objects. Selves that can stand back and see themselves having fun (an illusion which reassures them that they are real).

Such is the ignorance which is taken to be the axiomatic foundation of all knowledge in the human collectivity: in order to experience yourself as real, you have to suppress the awareness of your contingency, your unreality, your state of radical need. This you do by creating an awareness of yourself as *one who has no needs that he cannot immediately fulfill*. Basically, this is an illusion of omnipotence: an illusion which the collectivity arrogates to itself, and consents to share with its individual members in proportion as they submit to its more central and more rigid fabrications.

You have needs; but if you behave and conform you can participate in the collective power. You can then satisfy all your needs. Meanwhile, in order to increase its power over you, the collectivity increases your needs. It also tightens its demand for conformity. Thus you can become all the more committed to the collective illusion in proportion to becoming more hopelessly mortgaged to collective power.

How does this work? The collectivity informs and shapes your will to happiness ("have fun") by presenting you with irresistible images of yourself as you would like to be: having *fun that is so perfectly credible that it allows no interference of conscious doubt*. In theory such a good time can be so convincing that you are no longer aware of even a remote possibility that it might change into something less satisfying. In practice, expensive fun always admits of a doubt, which blossoms out into another full-blown need, which then calls for a still more credible and more costly refinement of satisfaction, which again fails you. The end of the cycle is despair.

Because we live in a womb of collective illusion, our

freedom remains abortive. Our capacities for joy, peace, and truth are never liberated. They can never be used. We are prisoners of a process, a dialectic of false promises and real deceptions ending in futility.

"The unborn child," says Philoxenos, "is already perfect and fully constituted in his nature, with all his senses, and limbs, but he cannot make use of them in their natural functions, because, in the womb, he cannot strengthen or develop them for such use."

Now, since all things have their season, there is a time to be unborn. We must begin, indeed, in the social womb. There is a time for warmth in the collective myth. But there is also a time to be born. He who is spiritually "born" as a mature identity is liberated from the enclosing womb of myth and prejudice. He learns to think for himself, guided no longer by the dictates of need and by the systems and processes designed to create artificial needs and then "satisfy" them.

This emancipation can take two forms: first that of the active life, which liberates itself from enslavement to necessity by considering and serving the needs of others, without thought of personal interest or return. And second, the contemplative life, which must not be construed as an escape from time and matter, from social responsibility and from the life of sense, but rather, as an advance into solitude and the desert, a confrontation with poverty and the void, a renunciation of the empirical self, in the presence of death, and nothingness, in order to overcome the ignorance and error that spring from the fear of "being nothing." The man who dares to be alone can come to see that the "emptiness" and "uselessness" which the collective mind fears and condemns are necessary conditions for the encounter with truth.

It is in the desert of loneliness and emptiness that the fear of death and the need for self-affirmation are seen to be illusory. When this is faced, then anguish is not necessarily overcome, but it can be accepted and understood. Thus, in the heart of anguish are found the gifts of peace and understanding: not simply in personal illumination and liberation, but by commitment and empathy, for the contemplative must assume the universal anguish and the inescapable condition of mortal man. The solitary, far from enclosing himself in himself, becomes every man. He dwells in the solitude, the poverty, the indigence of every man.

It is in this sense that the hermit, according to Philoxenos, imitates Christ. For in Christ, God takes to Himself the solitude and dereliction of man: every man. From the moment Christ went out into the desert to be tempted, the loneliness, the temptation and the hunger of every man became the loneliness, temptation and hunger of Christ. But in return, the gift of truth with which Christ dispelled the three kinds of illusion offered him in his temptation (security, reputation and power) can become also our own truth, if we can only accept it. It is offered to us also in temptation. "You too go out into the desert," said Philoxenos, "having with you

18

nothing of the world, and the Holy Spirit will go with you. See the freedom with which Jesus has gone forth, and go forth like Him—see where he has left the rule of men; leave the rule of the world where he has left the law, and go out with him to fight the power of error."

And where is the power of error? We find it was after all not in the city, but in *ourselves*.

TODAY the insights of a Philoxenos are to be sought less in the tracts of theologians than in the meditations of the existentialists and in the Theater of the Absurd. The problem of Berenger, in Ionesco's *Rhinoceros,* is the problem of the human person stranded and alone in what threatens to become a society of monsters. In the sixth century Berenger might perhaps have walked off into the desert of Scete, without too much concern over the fact that all his fellow citizens, all his friends, and even his girl Daisy, had turned into rhinoceroses.

The problem today is that there are no deserts, only dude ranches.

The desert islands are places where the wicked little characters in the *Lord of the Flies* come face to face with the Lord of the Flies, form a small, tight, ferocious collectivity of painted faces, and arm themselves with spears to hunt down the last member of their group who still remembers with nostalgia the possibilities of rational discourse.

When Berenger finds himself suddenly the last human in a rhinoceros herd he looks into the mirror and

19

says, humbly enough, "After all, man is not as bad as all that, is he?" But his world now shakes mightily with the stampede of his metamorphosed fellow citizens, and he soon becomes aware that the very stampede itself is the most telling and tragic of all arguments. For when he considers going out into the street "to try to convince them," he realizes that he "would have to learn their language." He looks in the mirror and sees that *he no longer resembles anyone*. He searches madly for a photograph of people as they were before the big change. But now humanity itself has become incredible, as well as hideous. To be the last man in the rhinoceros herd is, in fact, to be a monster.

Such is the problem which Ionesco sets us in his tragic irony: solitude and dissent become more and more impossible, more and more absurd. That Berenger finally accepts his absurdity and rushes out to challenge the whole herd only points up the futility of a commitment to rebellion. At the same time in *The New Tenant* (*Le Nouveau Locataire*) Ionesco portrays the absurdity of a logically consistent individualism which, in fact, is a self-isolation by the pseudo-logic of proliferating needs and possessions.

Ionesco protested that the New York production of *Rhinoceros* as a farce was a complete misunderstanding of his intention. It is a play not merely against *conformism* but about *totalitarianism*. The rhinoceros is not an amiable beast, and with him around the fun ceases and things begin to get serious. Everything has to make sense and be totally useful to the totally obsessive operation. At the same time Ionesco was criticized for not giving the audience "something positive" to take away with them, instead of just "refusing the human adventure." (Presumably "rhinoceritis" is the latest in human adventure!) He replied: "They [the spectators] leave in a void—and that was my intention. It is the business of a free man to pull himself out of this void by his own power and not by the power of other people!" In this Ionesco comes very close to Zen and to Christian eremitism.

"In all the cities of the world, it is the same," says Ionesco. "The universal and modern man is the man in a rush (i.e. a rhinoceros), a man who has no time, who is a prisoner of necessity, who cannot understand that *a thing might perhaps be without usefulness;* nor does he understand that, at bottom, it is the useful that may be a useless and back-breaking burden. If one does not understand the usefulness of the useless and the uselessness of the useful, one cannot understand art. And a country where art is not understood is a country of slaves and robots. . . ." (*Notes et Contre Notes,* p. 129) Rhinoceritis, he adds, is the sickness that lies in wait "for those who *have lost the sense and the taste for solitude.*"

The love of solitude is sometimes condemned as "hatred of our fellow men." But is this true? If we push our analysis of collective thinking a little further we will

21

find that the dialectic of power and need, of submission and satisfaction, ends by being a dialectic of hate. Collectivity needs not only to absorb everyone it can, but also implicitly to hate and destroy whoever cannot be absorbed. Paradoxically, one of the needs of collectivity is to reject certain classes, or races, or groups, in order to strengthen its own self-awareness by hating them instead of absorbing them.

Thus the solitary cannot survive unless he is capable of loving everyone, without concern for the fact that he is likely to be regarded by all of them as a traitor. Only the man who has fully attained his own spiritual identity can live without the need to kill, and without the need of a doctrine that permits him to do so with a good conscience. There will always be a place, says Ionesco, *"for those isolated consciences who have stood up for the universal conscience"* as against the mass mind. But their place is solitude. They have no other. Hence it is the solitary person (whether in the city or in the desert) who does mankind the inestimable favor of reminding it of its true capacity for maturity, liberty and peace.

It sounds very much like Philoxenos to me.

And it sounds like what the rain says. We still carry this burden of illusion because we do not dare to lay it down. We suffer all the needs that society demands we suffer, because if we do not have these needs we lose our "usefulness" in society—the usefulness of suckers. We fear to be alone, and to be ourselves, and so to remind others of the truth that is in them.

22

"I will not make you such rich men as have need of many things," said Philoxenos (putting the words on the lips of Christ), "but I will make you true rich men who have need of nothing. Since it is not he who has many possessions that is rich, but he who has no needs." Obviously, we shall always have *some* needs. But only he who has the simplest and most natural needs can be considered to be without needs, since the only needs he has are real ones, and the real ones are not hard to fulfill if one is a free man!

THE rain has stopped. The afternoon sun slants through the pine trees: and how those useless needles smell in the clear air!

A dandelion, long out of season, has pushed itself into bloom between the smashed leaves of last summer's day lilies. The valley resounds with the totally uninformative talk of creeks and wild water.

Then the quails begin their sweet whistling in the wet bushes. Their noise is absolutely useless, and so is the delight I take in it. There is nothing I would rather hear, not because it is a better noise than other noises, but because it is the voice of the present moment, the present festival.

Yet even here the earth shakes. Over at Fort Knox the Rhinoceros is having fun.

To Each His Darkness

Chaque homme dans sa nuit —
NOTES ON A NOVEL OF JULIEN GREEN.

JULIEN GREEN creates a world of closely enmeshed contradictions: the young man who is regarded as devout,
and is impure. The death of the impure old man "covered with Latin prayers." The horrid puritan who inflicts
his determined will, his upright conscience on everyone,
who is gifted with a frightful insight. He is hateful, yet
can he after all be right?

A constant uncertainty: that which is absolutely
worst must soon happen?

That which is most dreadful must after all turn out
to be true?

The worst is never absolutely certain, and yet as we
move along one evil possibility after another becomes
certain and we are left with the final uncertainty—the
one that cannot be resolved in a book or in this life—
the last question: whether the final awful possibility,
that of damnation, may turn out also to have been certain from the beginning, inflicted by an inexorable will.

The awful ease with which seduction takes place,

27

not because it is desired but rather, perhaps, because it is part of an inexorable pattern from which there can be no escape.

The *inexorable consistency* of this world of fear!

A dream, a nightmare has that same consistency until we wake up. We can say: "But after all *he made this up!*" Yet we ask, in the end, if that explains anything. Maybe. . .? His talent is to leave us with the tantalizing question which is his own torment.

What is the question? Salvation, damnation? or is it the question: *What is serious? What is really to be taken seriously?* What is the meaning of seriousness? What is to be doubted? What is to be dismissed as not serious? Is there *anything serious?* Is there *anything not serious?* It is perhaps the question of reality itself.

Hence he creates this awful consistent universe in which everything *may be* serious, very serious, vitally serious. Every little thing, every movement of a blade of grass in the wind may turn out to have been so serious that your whole destiny depended on it.

Is destiny serious? This he seems not to question.

Sometimes I ask myself whether Green's sense of guilt, his shame at his creative gift—a deeply religious shame in a way, as if God should be the only one with *any* kind of creativity—does not lead him to question the very structure of reality. Is "reality" itself only the false floor over an infinite void?

His gift enables him to conjure up people in a world

of sin and drives him to damn them. Is creativity itself shot through with destruction, because it is from Eros, and Eros is also full of death? But if this is the question it implies a profound distrust of God Himself. It suggests terrible analogies. It seems to imitate what He might do with His creative power. If He creates, is it only in order to destroy? Here we have the dilemma of the artist in Green: his fear of his own creative gift, his temptation to mistrust the danger of his art because he can never forget for one moment that it is rooted in Eros.

Is this the world of religion, or of magic?

There is, there should be, in religion, the power of magic, but transformed, transfigured, exorcised, clean, free.

We know we are never free from magic, never entirely free from obsession. To treat religion as if it could be entirely clear of obsession is, in one sweep, to rob it of all its seriousness (until the spirit of God delivers us Himself from our obsessions).

Yet when everything is serious, perhaps nothing is serious: since seriousness is relative, to destroy the relationship is to destroy seriousness.

Green makes relationship inexorable.

In this world it is terrible how things "hang together."

The enmeshing of passions, flame within flame, nets and ropes of fire that is pleasure, the world nested in a moving mesh of unending fire, passion, passion, passion! The consistency of the *massa damnata* in which all are dragged down into hell and *no one* is surely saved: neither the Calvinist with his grim determination that others should be damned, nor the priest with his impatient will that all should have been rescued by a sacrament, *ex opere operato*—since that is the business of a priest.

But where are they?

Is it enough that they have the will to be saved?

And to have the will to be saved, must one limit oneself very carefully *to a few select things that are taken seriously*? And must everything else be ignored? In other words, to be saved is to exclude from consideration the possibility that one might be damned?

To take that possibility of damnation seriously is, then, to be lost?

But how do anything else? How *not* take it seriously?

(Think of the unspeakable triviality of popular religion which consists in *not* taking the possibility of damnation seriously any more!

To be saved, is then, to be rescued from seriousness!

To fall into the ludicrous and satanic flippancy of false piety, *kitsch,* Saint Sulpice!—or the euphoria of busy and optimistic groups!)

So, unless you can falsify and dominate reality with will, you are lost—and if you can impose your own obsession on reality (instead of having reality impose itself as an obsession *on you*) then are you perhaps doubly lost?

The question of this book, the deeper question, is the very nature of reality itself.

Inexorable consistency. Is reality the same as consistency?

The "reality" of the world he creates is made of consistency, but the reality of the real world is not consistent.

The world of consistency is the world of justice, but justice is not the final word.

There is, above the consistent and the logical world of justice, an inconsistent illogical world where nothing "hangs together," where justice no longer damns each man to his own darkness. This inconsistent world is the realm of mercy.

The world can only be "consistent" *without God*.

His freedom will always threaten it with inconsistency—with unexpected gifts.

A god who is fitted into our world scheme in order to make it serious and consistent is *not God*.

Such a world is not to be taken seriously, such a god is not to be taken seriously. If such a god is "absent" then doubtless the absence is a blessing.

To take him seriously is to submit to obsession, to doubt, to magic, and then to escape these, or try to escape them, by willfulness, by the determination to stake all on an arbitrary selection of "things to be taken seriously" because they "save," because they are "his affairs."

(Note that even atheism takes seriously this god of consistency).

But mercy breaks into the world of magic and justice and overturns its apparent consistency. Mercy is inconsistent. It is therefore comic. It liberates us from the tragic seriousness of the obsessive world which we have "made up" for ourselves by yielding to our obsessions. Only mercy can liberate us from the madness of our determination to be consistent—from the awful pattern of lusts, greeds, angers and hatreds which mix us up together like a mass of dough and thrust us all together into the oven.

Mercy cannot be contained in the web of obsessions.

Nor is it something one determines to think about—that one resolves to "take seriously," in the sense of becoming obsessed with it.

You cannot become obsessed with mercy!

This is the inner secret of mercy. It is totally incompatible with obsession, with compulsion. It liberates from all the rigid and deterministic structures which magic strives to impose on reality (or which science, the child of magic, tries to impose)!

Mercy is not to be purchased by a set way of acting, by a formal determination to be consistent.

Law is consistent. Grace is "inconsistent."

The Cross is the sign of contradiction—destroying the seriousness of the Law, of the Empire, of the armies, of blood sacrifice, and of obsession.

32

But the magicians keep turning the Cross to their own purposes. Yes, it is for them too a sign of contradiction: the awful blasphemy of the religious magician who *makes the Cross contradict mercy!* This of course is the ultimate temptation of Christianity! To say that Christ has locked all the doors, has given one answer, settled everything and departed, leaving all life enclosed in the frightful consistency of a system outside of which there is *seriousness and damnation,* inside of which there is the intolerable flippancy of the saved—while nowhere is there any place left for the mystery of the freedom of divine mercy which alone is truly serious, and worthy of being taken seriously.

33

Flannery O'Connor:
a Prose Elegy

Now Flannery is dead and I will write her name with honor, with love for the great slashing innocence of that dry-eyed irony that could keep looking the South in the face without bleeding or even sobbing. Her South was deeper than mine, crazier than Kentucky, but wild with no other madness than the crafty paranoia that is all over the place, including the North! Only madder, craftier, hung up in wilder and more absurd legends, more inventive of more outrageous lies! And solemn! Taking seriously the need to be respectable when one is an obsolescent and very agile fury.

The key word to Flannery's stories probably is "respect." She never gave up examining its ambiguities and its decay. In this bitter dialectic of half-truths that have become endemic to our system, she probed our very life—its conflicts, its falsities, its obsessions, its vanities. Have we become an enormous complex organization of spurious reverences? Respect is continually advertised, and we are still convinced that we respect "everything good"—when we know too well that we have lost the most elementary respect even for ourselves. Flannery saw this and saw, better than others, what it implied.

She wrote in and out of the anatomy of a word that became genteel, then self-conscious, then obsessive, finally dying of contempt, but kept calling itself "respect." Contempt for the child, for the stranger, for the woman, for the Negro, for the animal, for the white man, for the farmer, for the country, for the preacher, for the city, for the world, for reality itself. Contempt, contempt, so that in the end the gestures of respect they kept making to themselves and to each other and to God became desperately obscene.

But respect had to be maintained. Flannery maintained it ironically and relentlessly with a kind of innocent passion long after it had died of contempt —as if she were the only one left who took this thing seriously. One would think (if one put a Catholic chip on his shoulder and decided to make a problem of her) that she could not look so steadily, so drily and so long at so much false respect without herself dying of despair. She never made any funny faces. She never said: "Here is a terrible thing!" She just looked and said what they said and how they said it. It was not she that invented their despair, and perhaps her only way out of despair herself was to respect the way they announced the gospel of contempt. She patiently recorded all they had got themselves into.

Their world was a big, fantastic, crawling, exploding junk pile of despair. I will write her name with honor for seeing it so clearly and looking straight at it without remorse. Perhaps her way of irony was the only possible catharsis for a madness so cruel and so endemic. Perhaps a dry honesty like hers can save the South more simply than the North can ever be saved.

Flannery's people were two kinds of very advanced primitives: the city kind, exhausted, disillusioned, tired of imagining, perhaps still given to a grim willfulness in the service of doubt, still driving on in fury and ill will, or scientifically expert in nastiness; and the rural kind: furious, slow, cunning, inexhaustible, living sweetly on the verge of the unbelievable, more inclined to prefer the abyss to solid ground, but keeping contact with the world of contempt by raw insensate poetry and religious mirth: the mirth of a god who himself, they suspected, was the craftiest and most powerful deceiver of all. Flannery saw the contempt of primitives who admitted that they would hate to be saved, and the greater contempt of those other primitives whose salvation was an elaborately contrived possibility, always being brought back into question. Take the sweet idiot deceit of the fury grandmother in "A Good Man Is Hard to Find" whose respectable and catastrophic fantasy easily destroyed her urban son with all his plans, his last shred of trust in reason, and his insolent children.

The way Flannery O'Connor made a story: she would

39

put together all these elements of unreason and let them fly slowly and inexorably at one another. Then sometimes the urban madness, less powerful, would fall weakly prey to the rural madness and be inexorably devoured by a superior and more primitive absurdity. Or the rural madness would fail and fall short of the required malice and urban deceit would compass its destruction, with all possible contempt, cursing, superior violence and fully implemented disbelief. For it would usually be wholesome faith that left the rural primitive unarmed. So you would watch, fascinated, almost in despair, knowing that in the end the very worst thing, the least reasonable, the least desirable, was what would have to happen. Not because Flannery wanted it so, but because it turned out to *be* so in a realm where the advertised satisfaction is compounded of so many lies and of so much contempt for the customer. She had seen too clearly all that is sinister in our commercial paradise, and in its rural roots.

Flannery's people were two kinds of trash, able to mix inanity with poetry, with exuberant nonsense, and with the most profound and systematic contempt for reality. Her people knew how to be trash to the limit, unabashed, on purpose, out of self-contempt that has finally won out over every other feeling and turned into a parody of freedom in the spirit. What spirit? A spirit of ungodly stateliness and parody—the pomp and glee of arbitrary sports, freaks not of nature but of blighted and social willfulness, rich in the creation of respectable and three-eyed monsters. Her beings are always raising the question of *worth*. Who is a good man? Where is he? He is "hard to find." Meanwhile you will have to make out with a bad one who is so respectable that he is horrible, so horrible that he is funny, so funny that he is pathetic, but so pathetic that it would be gruesome to pity him. So funny that you do not dare to laugh too loud for fear of demons.

And that is how Flannery finally solved the problem of respect: having peeled the whole onion of respect layer by layer, having taken it all apart with admirable patience, showing clearly that each layer was only another kind of contempt, she ended up by seeing clearly that it was funny, but not merely funny in a way that you could laugh at. Humorous, yes, but also uncanny, inexplicable, demonic, so you could never laugh at it as if you understood. Because if you pretended to understand, you, too, would find yourself among her demons practicing contempt. She respected all her people by searching for some sense in them, searching for truth, searching to the end and then suspending judgment. To have condemned them on moral grounds would have been to connive with their own crafty arts and their own demonic imagination. It would have meant getting tangled up with them in the same machinery of unreality and of contempt. The only way to be saved was to stay out of it, not to think, not to speak, just to record the slow, sweet, ridiculous verbalizing of Southern furies, working their way through their charming lazy hell.

That is why when I read Flannery I don't think of Hemingway, or Katherine Anne Porter, or Sartre, but rather of someone like Sophocles. What more can be said of a writer? I write her name with honor, for all the truth and all the craft with which she shows man's fall and his dishonor.

A Devout Meditation
in Memory of
Adolf Eichmann

ONE of the most disturbing facts that came out in the
Eichmann trial was that a psychiatrist examined him
and pronounced him *perfectly sane*. I do not doubt it
at all, and that is precisely why I find it disturbing.

If all the Nazis had been psychotics, as some of their
leaders probably were, their appalling cruelty would
have been in some sense easier to understand. It is much
worse to consider this calm, "well-balanced," unper-
turbed official conscientiously going about his desk
work, his administrative job which happened to be the
supervision of mass murder. He was thoughtful, orderly,
unimaginative. He had a profound respect for system,
for law and order. He was obedient, loyal, a faithful
officer of a great state. He served his government very
well.

He was not bothered much by guilt. I have not heard
that he developed any psychosomatic illnesses. Apparently he slept well. He had a good appetite, or so it

45

seems. True, when he visited Auschwitz, the Camp Commandant, Hoess, in a spirit of sly deviltry, tried to tease the big boss and scare him with some of the sights. Eichmann was disturbed, yes. He was disturbed. Even Himmler had been disturbed, and had gone weak at the knees. Perhaps, in the same way, the general manager of a big steel mill might be disturbed if an accident took place while he happened to be somewhere in the plant. But of course what happened at Auschwitz was not an accident: just the routine unpleasantness of the daily task. One must shoulder the burden of daily monotonous work for the Fatherland. Yes, one must suffer discomfort and even nausea from unpleasant sights and sounds. It all comes under the heading of duty, self-sacrifice, and obedience. Eichmann was devoted to duty, and proud of his job.

The sanity of Eichmann is disturbing. We equate sanity with a sense of justice, with humaneness, with prudence, with the capacity to love and understand other people. We rely on the sane people of the world to preserve it from barbarism, madness, destruction. And now it begins to dawn on us that it is precisely the *sane* ones who are the most dangerous.

It is the sane ones, the well-adapted ones, who can without qualms and without nausea aim the missiles and press the buttons that will initiate the great festival of destruction that they, *the sane ones,* have prepared. What makes us so sure, after all, that the danger comes from a psychotic getting into a position to fire the first shot in a nuclear war? Psychotics will be suspect. The sane ones will keep them far from the button. No one suspects the sane, and the sane ones will have *perfectly good reasons*, logical, well-adjusted reasons, for firing the shot. They will be obeying sane orders that have come sanely down the chain of command. And because of their sanity they will have no qualms at all. When the missiles take off, then, *it will be no mistake*.

We can no longer assume that because a man is "sane" he is therefore in his "right mind." The whole concept of sanity in a society where spiritual values have lost their meaning is itself meaningless. A man can be "sane" in the limited sense that he is not impeded by his disordered emotions from acting in a cool, orderly manner, according to the needs and dictates of the social situation in which he finds himself. He can be perfectly "adjusted." God knows, perhaps such people can be perfectly adjusted even in hell itself.

And so I ask myself: what is the meaning of a concept of sanity that excludes love, considers it irrelevant, and destroys our capacity to love other human beings, to respond to their needs and their sufferings, to recognize them also as persons, to apprehend their pain as one's own? Evidently this is not necessary for "sanity" at all. It is a religious notion, a spiritual notion, a Christian notion. What business have we to equate "sanity" with "Christianity"? None at all, obviously. The worst error

47

is to imagine that a Christian must try to be "sane" like everybody else, that we *belong* in our kind of *society*. That we must be "realistic" about it. We must develop a *sane* Christianity: and there have been plenty of sane Christians in the past. Torture is nothing new, is it? We ought to be able to rationalize a little brainwashing, and genocide, and find a place for nuclear war, or at least for napalm bombs, in our moral theology. Certainly some of us are doing our best along those lines already. There are hopes! Even Christians can shake off their sentimental prejudices about charity, and become sane like Eichmann. They can even cling to a certain set of Christian formulas, and fit them into a Totalist Ideology. Let them talk about justice, charity, love, and the rest. These words have not stopped some sane men from acting very sanely and cleverly in the past. . . .

No, Eichmann was sane. The generals and fighters on both sides, in World War II, the ones who carried out the total destruction of entire cities, these were the sane ones. Those who have invented and developed atomic bombs, thermonuclear bombs, missiles; who have planned the strategy of the next war; who have evaluated the various possibilities of using bacterial and chemical agents: these are not the crazy people, they are the *sane* people. The ones who coolly estimate how many millions of victims can be considered expendable in a nuclear war, I presume they do all right with the Rorschach ink blots too. On the other hand, you will probably find that the pacifists and the ban-the-bomb people are, quite seriously, just as we read in *Time,* a little crazy.

I am beginning to realize that "sanity" is no longer a value or an end in itself. The "sanity" of modern man is about as useful to him as the huge bulk and muscles of the dinosaur. If he were a little less sane, a little more doubtful, a little more aware of his absurdities and contradictions, perhaps there might be a possibility of his survival. But if he is sane, too sane . . . perhaps we must say that in a society like ours the worst insanity is to be totally without anxiety, totally "sane."

Letter to an Innocent
Bystander

IF I dare, in these few words, to ask you some direct and personal questions, it is because I address them as much to myself as to you. It is because I am still able to hope that a civil exchange of ideas can take place between two persons—that we have not yet reached the stage where we are all hermetically sealed, each one in the collective arrogance and despair of his own herd. If I seem to be in a hurry to take advantage of the situation that still exists, it is, frankly, because I sometimes feel it may not continue to exist much longer. In any case, I believe that we are still sufficiently "persons" to realize we have a common difficulty, and to try to solve it together. I write this, then, in the hope that we can still save ourselves from becoming numbers.

You can easily guess that in using the term "innocent bystander" I had to examine my conscience to see whether or not I was being facetious. I do not remember if I smiled when I first thought of it, but in any case I am no longer smiling. For I do not think the question of our innocence can be a matter for jesting, and I am no longer certain that it is honorable to stand by as the helpless witness of a cataclysm, with no other hope than to die innocently and by accident, as a non-participant.

But who are "we"? We are the intellectuals who have taken for granted that we could be "bystanders" and that our quality as detached observers could preserve our innocence and relieve us of responsibility. By intellectual, I do not mean clerk (though I might mean *clerc*). I do not mean bureaucrat. I do not mean politician. I do not mean technician. I do not mean anyone whose intelligence ministers to a machine for counting, classifying, and distributing other people: who hands out to this one a higher pay check and to that one a trip (presently) to the forced labor camp. I do not mean a policeman, or a propagandist. I still dare to use the word intellectual as if it had a meaning.

So here we stand, you and I, while "they" attend to their increasingly sinister affairs, and we observe: "Well, let others mind their own business and we will mind ours." Such an attitude soon leads to another, hardly innocent, in which we may find ourselves saying: "You can't make an omelet without breaking eggs." From this it is but one step to a doctrine even more timely and more consoling: "You can't break eggs without making an omelet." If you have already got that far there is no use in reading any more of this letter.

This inspires me to ask my first dangerous question.

54

"Although it seems to be impossible to do anything but stand and wait, is our waiting harmless, and is it innocent? Can we afford to remain inert? Can we afford to confuse helplessness with honesty? It is true that if one is helpless, honesty requires that he admit it. But if he is helpless through his own neglect, he can hardly permit himself to be complacent in an admission of helplessness that is not, at the same time, an admission of guilt."

You will answer: "Waiting is not inertia. To be quiet and bide one's time is to resist. Passive resistance is a form of action."

That is true when one is waiting for something, and knows for what he is waiting. That is true when one is resisting, and knows why, and to what end, he is resisting, and whom he must resist. Unless our waiting implies knowledge and action, we will find ourselves waiting for our own destruction and nothing more. A witness of a crime, who just stands by and makes a mental note of the fact that he is an innocent bystander, tends by that very fact to become an accomplice.

Are we waiting for anything? Do we stand for anything? Do we know what we want?

Here we stand, in a state of diffuse irritation and doubt, while "they" fight one another for power over the whole world. It is our confusion that enables "them" to use us, and to pit us against one another, for their own purposes. Our guilt, our deep resentment, do nothing to preserve us from a shameful fate. On the contrary, our resentment is what fits us most perfectly to be "their" instruments. How can we claim that our inertia is innocent? It is the source of our guilt.

Is non-participation possible? Can complicity be avoided? You in your country and I in mine—you in your circle and I in my monastery: does the fact that we hate and resent tyranny and try to dissociate ourselves from it suffice to keep us innocent?

First, let us assume that we are clear who "they" are. When I speak of "them," you will understand that I mean those special ones who seek power over "all the others," and who use us as instruments to gain power over the others. Thus there are three groups I am thinking of: "they," "we" and "the others." We, the intellectuals, stand in the middle, and we must not forget that, in the end, everything depends on *us*.

It is therefore supremely important for us not to yield to despair, abandon ourselves to the "inevitable" and identify ourselves with "them." Our duty is to refuse to believe that their way is "inevitable." And it is equally important for us not to set ourselves too exclusively apart from "the others" who depend on us, and upon whom we ourselves also depend.

As for the powerful ones, it is our job to recognize them even without their police, even before the establishment of their machinery. We must identify them wherever "they" may appear, even though they may rise up in the midst of ourselves, or among "the others." We must be able to recognize "them" by what they *are* and not rest satisfied with what is said about them, by others or by themselves or above all by one of us! It is already rare for an intellectual to retain his sense of judgment when "they" change their masks and reshuffle their labels and put on different badges. Yet "they" are always "they." It is to their obvious interest to bribe us to give them a new name, a false identity, especially since, in doing so, we convince ourselves that we have made a brilliant discovery. We must not let our vanity provide "them" with false passports.

Let us assume, at this point, that we are not interested in their money, or their official benevolence, or their protection, or the cushy state jobs which they can guarantee us, if we will place our resentment at their service. Needless to say, I have assumed too much. We *are* interested, aren't we? Let's not use that nasty word "prostitution" though. The situation is already depressing enough without self-disparagement. . . .

In any case, as we "wait" we must make sure they do not, once again, convince us that it is "they" we have been waiting for.

A second thought. Before we try to decide what we are waiting for, let us make sure whether or not we are *waiting*. Perhaps, indeed, we have already given up hope of anything else. Perhaps we are unconsciously very busy in preparing the way for something which, in our right minds, we would be the last to wait for. In that case, not only are we not waiting for salvation, we are actively preparing our own destruction.

This leads to a third question. Forgive me for asking: but do we not, after all, *prefer* to be frustrated and led into despair? Are we not content to make despair a comfortable evasion—since it has certain elements of the picturesque—and by despair do we not come to terms with the meaninglessness of our own existence? Despair indeed seems very respectable, until one remembers that this is only the preparation to accept "their" next formula, which will explain, and exploit, our emptiness.

For you see, our emptiness is not innocent, not simply neutral, not "nothing." Our self-hatred is anything but contrition. It is the terrible spiritual vacuum into which malevolence can, like lightning, introduce itself in order to produce a universal explosion of hatred and destruction. This explosion is made possible by *our* emptiness. Without us, the emptiness of all the others would never be activated, and the death that sleeps in them would never be able to leap out and smash everything in sight.

And that reminds me of another thing: When we "stand by" we try to think of ourselves as independent, as standing on our own feet. It is true that as intellectuals we ought to stand on our own feet—but one cannot learn to do this until he has first recognized to what extent he requires the support of the others. And it is our business to support one another against "them," not to be supported by "them" and used to crush "the others."

"They," of course, have never really been in any position to support anyone. "They" need us, but not our strength. They do not want us strong, but weak. It is our emptiness "they" need, as a justification of their own emptiness. That is why their support comes always, and only, in the form of bribes. We are nourished in order that we may continue to sleep. We are paid to keep quiet, or to say things that do not disturb the unruffled surface of that emptiness from which, in due time, the spark and the blast must leap out and release, in all men, the grand explosion.

And now the last question. It is the one you will probably like least of all. But I must ask it. Do we have any choice left? Do we not have to march where all the others march, and shout as madly as they? Worse still: are we not the kind of bystanders whose very "innocence" makes them guilty, makes them the obvious target for arbitrary terror?

If that is the case, and if we are able dimly to realize what it means, we shall almost certainly fail to resist the last and most degrading temptation: the temptation of the innocent intellectual who rushes frantically into collaboration with "them," lends himself to every defilement, *certain* that he is being prepared for destruction, and, in the end, asking only to be defiled as often and as sordidly as possible before the final annihilation takes place.

It is this that I fear for both of us: the frantic insistence on getting rid even of our innocence, as if any other guilt would be more bearable, in such a world, than the guilt of being innocent.

When all this has been said, and pondered by us both, I think you would take it as bad manners for me to offer an easy solution. And I am hardly mad enough to try it. I love you enough (the word "love" slipped out by mistake) to spare your legitimate pride. It is not for me to provide the same kind of clear, sweeping program of action which is "their" great temptation and their delusion. The very difficulty of our position comes from the fact that every definite program is now a deception, every precise plan is a trap, every easy solution is intellectual suicide. And that is why we are caught on the horns of a dilemma: whether we "act" or not we are likely to be destroyed. There is a certain innocence in not having a solution. There is a certain innocence in a kind of despair: but only if in despair we find salvation. I mean, despair of this world and what is in it. Despair of men and of their plans, in order to hope for the impossible answer that lies beyond our earthly contradictions, and yet can burst into our world and solve them if only there are some who hope in spite of despair.

The true solutions are not those which we force upon life in accordance with our theories, but those which life itself provides for those who dispose themselves to receive the truth. Consequently our task is to dissociate ourselves from all who have theories which promise clear-cut and infallible solutions, and to mistrust all such theories, not in a spirit of negativism and defeat, but rather trusting life itself, and nature, and if you will permit me, God above all. For since man has decided to occupy the place of God he has shown himself to be by far the blindest, and cruelest, and pettiest and most ridiculous of all the false gods. We can call ourselves innocent only if we refuse to forget this, and if we also do everything we can to make others realize it.

To illustrate what I mean, I will remind you of an innocent and ancient story, of a king and his new clothes.

You know it, of course. It has been referred to somewhere in psychoanalytical literature. Tailors deceived a king, telling them they would weave him a wonderful suit which would be invisible to any but good men. They went through all the motions of fitting him out in the invisible suit, and the king, as well as all his courtiers claimed to "see" and to admire the thing. In the end the naked king paraded out into the street where all the people were gathered to admire his suit of clothes, and all did admire it until a child dared to point out that the king was naked.

You will perhaps find that my thought has taken on a sentimental tinge. But since the times have become what they have become, I dare to blurt this out. Have you and I forgotten that our vocation, as innocent bystanders—and the very condition of our terrible innocence—is to do what the child did, and keep on saying the king is naked, at the cost of being condemned criminals? Remember, the child in the tale was the only innocent one: and because of his innocence, the fault of the others was kept from being criminal, and was nothing worse than foolishness. If the child had not been there, they would all have been madmen, or criminals. It was the child's cry that saved them.

The Time of the End
Is the Time of No Room

NOTE: In its Biblical sense, the expression "the End" does not necessarily mean only "the violent, sudden and bad end." Biblical eschatology must not be confused with the vague and anxious eschatology of human foreboding. We live in an age of two superimposed eschatologies: that of secular anxieties and hopes, and that of revealed fulfillment. Sometimes the first is merely mistaken for the second, sometimes it results from complete denial and despair of the second. In point of fact the pathological *fear of the violent end* which, when sufficiently aroused, actually becomes a thinly disguised *hope for the violent end*, provides something of the climate of confusion and despair in which the more profound hopes of Biblical eschatology are realized—for everyone is forced to confront the *possibility,* and to accept or reject them. This definitive confrontation is precisely what Biblical eschatology announces to us. In speaking of "the time of the End," we keep in mind both these levels of meaning. But it should be clear that for the author, there is no question of prognostication or Apocalypse—only a sober statement about the climate of our time, a time of finality and of fulfillment.

WHEN the perfect and ultimate message, the joy which is *The Great Joy,* explodes silently upon the world, there is no longer any room for sadness. Therefore no circumstance in the Christmas Gospel, however trivial it may seem, is to be left out of The Great Joy. In the special and heavenly light which shines around the coming of the Word into the world, all ordinary things are transfigured. In the mystery of Peace which is proclaimed to a world that cannot believe in peace, a world of suspicion, hatred and distrust, even the rejection of the Prince of Peace takes on something of the color and atmosphere of peace.

So there was no room at the inn? True! But that is simply mentioned in passing, in a matter of fact sort of way, as the Evangelist points to what he really means us to see—the picture of pure peace, pure joy: "She wrapped her first born Son in swaddling clothes and laid him in the manger" (Luke 2:7). By now we know it well, and yet we all might still be questioning it—except that a reason was given for an act that might otherwise have seemed strange: "there was no room for them at the inn." Well, then, they obviously found some other place!

But when we read the Gospels and come to know them thoroughly, we realize there are other reasons why it was necessary that there be no room at the inn, and why there had to be some other place. In fact, the inn was the last place in the world for the birth of the Lord.

The Evangelists, preparing us for the announcement of the birth of the Lord, remind us that the fullness of time has come. Now is the time of final decision, the time of mercy, the "acceptable time," the time of settlement, the time of the end. It is the time of repentance, the time for the fulfillment of all promises, for the Promised One has come. But with the coming of the end, a great bustle and business begins to shake the nations of the world. The time of the end is the time of massed armies, "wars and rumors of wars," of huge crowds moving this way and that, of "men withering away for fear," of flaming cities and sinking fleets, of smoking lands laid waste, of technicians planning grandiose acts of destruction. The time of the end is the time of the Crowd: and the eschatological message is spoken in a world where, precisely because of the vast indefinite roar of armies on the move and the restlessness of turbulent mobs, the message can be heard only with difficulty. Yet it is heard by those who are aware that the display of power, *hubris* and destruction is part of the *kerygma*. That which is to be judged announces itself, introduces itself by its sinister and arrogant claim to absolute power. Thus it is identified, and those who decide in favor of this claim are numbered, marked with the sign of power, aligned with power, and destroyed with it.

Why then was the inn crowded? Because of the census, the eschatological massing of the *"whole world"* in centers of registration, to be numbered, to be identified with the structure of imperial power. The purpose of the census: to discover those who were to be taxed. To find out those who were eligible for service in the armies of the empire.

The Bible had not been friendly to a census in the days when God was the ruler of Israel (II Samuel 24).

67

The numbering of the people of God by an alien emperor and their full consent to it was itself an eschatological sign, preparing those who could understand it to meet judgment with repentance. After all, in the Apocalyptic literature of the Bible, this "summoning together" or convocation of the powers of the earth to do battle is the great sign of "the end." For then "the demon spirits that work wonders go out to the Kings all over the world to muster them for battle on the great Day of God Almighty" (Revelations 16:14). And "the Beasts and the Kings of the earth and their armies gathered to make war upon him who was mounted on the horse and on his army" (Revelations 19:19). Then all the birds of prey gather from all sides in response to the angel's cry: "Gather for God's great banquet, and eat the bodies of Kings, commanders and mighty men, of horses and their riders . . ." (Revelations 19:18).

It was therefore impossible that the Word should lose Himself by being born into shapeless and passive mass. He had indeed emptied Himself, taken the form of God's servant, man. But he did not empty Himself to the point of becoming mass man, faceless man. It was therefore right that there should be no room for him in a crowd that had been called together as an eschatological sign. His being born outside that crowd is even more of a sign. That there is no room for Him is a sign of the end.

Nor are the tidings of great joy announced in the

68

crowded inn. In the massed crowd there are always new tidings of joy and disaster. Where each new announcement is the greatest of announcements, where every day's disaster is beyond compare, every day's danger demands the ultimate sacrifice, all news and all judgment is reduced to zero. News becomes merely a new noise in the mind, briefly replacing the noise that went before it and yielding to the noise that comes after it, so that eventually everything blends into the same monotonous and meaningless rumor. News? There is so much news that there is no room left for the true tidings, the "Good News," *The Great Joy.*

Hence The Great Joy is announced, after all, in silence, loneliness and darkness, to shepherds "living in the fields" or "living in the countryside" and apparently unmoved by the rumors or massed crowds. These are the remnant of the desert-dwellers, the nomads, the true Israel.

Even though "the whole world" is ordered to be inscribed, they do not seem to be affected. Doubtless they have registered, as Joseph and Mary will register, but they remain outside the agitation, and untouched by the vast movement, the massing of hundreds and thousands of people everywhere in the towns and cities.

They are therefore quite otherwise signed. They are designated, surrounded by a great light, they receive the message of The Great Joy, and they believe it with joy. They see the Shekinah over them, recognize themselves for what they are. They are the remnant, the people of no account, who are therefore chosen—the *anawim*. And they obey the light. Nor was anything else asked of them.

They go and they see not a prophet, not a spirit, but the Flesh in which the glory of the Lord will be revealed and by which all men will be delivered from the power that is in the world, the power that seeks to destroy the world because the world is God's creation, the power that mimics creation, and in doing so, pillages and exhausts the resources of a bounteous God-given earth.

We live in the time of no room, which is the time of the end. The time when everyone is obsessed with lack of time, lack of space, with saving time, conquering space, projecting into time and space the anguish produced within them by the technological furies of size, volume, quantity, speed, number, price, power and acceleration.

The primordial blessing, "increase and multiply," has suddenly become a hemorrhage of terror. We are numbered in billions, and massed together, marshalled, numbered, marched here and there, taxed, drilled, armed, worked to the point of insensibility, dazed by information, drugged by entertainment, surfeited with everything, nauseated with the human race and with ourselves, nauseated with life.

As the end approaches, there is no room for nature. The cities crowd it off the face of the earth.

As the end approaches, there is no room for quiet. There is no room for solitude. There is no room for thought. There is no room for attention, for the awareness of our state.

In the time of the ultimate end, there is no room for man.

Those that lament the fact that there is no room for God must also be called to account for this. Have they perhaps added to the general crush by preaching a solid marble God that makes man alien to himself, a God that settles himself grimly like an implacable object in the inner heart of man and drives man out of himself in despair?

The time of the end is the time of demons who occupy the heart (pretending to be gods) so that man himself finds no room for himself in himself. He finds no space to rest in his own heart, not because it is full, but because it is void. Yet if he knew that the void itself, when hovered over by the Spirit, is an abyss of creativity. . . . He cannot believe it. There is no room for belief.

There is no room for him in the massed crowds of the eschatological society, the society of the end, in which all those for whom there is no room are thrown together, thrust, pitched out bodily into a whirlpool of empty forms, human specters, swirling aimlessly through their cities, *all wishing they had never been born.*

In the time of the end there is no longer room for the

desire to go on living. The time of the end is the time when men call upon the mountains to fall upon them, because they wish they did not exist.

Why? Because they are part of a proliferation of life that is not fully alive, it is programmed for death. A life that has not been chosen, and can hardly be accepted, has no more room for hope. Yet it must pretend to go on hoping. It is haunted by the demon of emptiness. And out of this unutterable void come the armies, the missiles, the weapons, the bombs, the concentration camps, the race riots, the racist murders, and all the other crimes of mass society.

Is this pessimism? Is this the unforgivable sin of admitting what everybody really feels? Is it pessimism to diagnose cancer as cancer? Or should one simply go on pretending that everything is getting better every day, because the time of the end is also—for some at any rate—the time of great prosperity? ("The Kings of the earth have joined in her idolatry and the traders of the earth have grown rich from her excessive luxury" (Revelations 18:3).

Into this world, this demented inn, in which there is absolutely no room for Him at all, Christ has come uninvited. But because He cannot be at home in it, because He is out of place in it, and yet He must be in it, His place is with those others for whom there is no room. His place is with those who do not belong, who are rejected by power because they are regarded as weak, those who are discredited, who are denied the status of persons, tortured, exterminated. With those for whom there is no room, Christ is present in this world. He is mysteriously present in those for whom there seems to be nothing but the world at its worst. For them, there is no escape even in imagination. They cannot identify with the power structure of a crowded humanity which seeks to project itself outward, anywhere, in a centrifugal flight into the void, to get *out there* where there is no God, no man, no name, no identity, no weight, no self, nothing but the bright, self-directed, perfectly obedient and infinitely expensive machine.

For those who are stubborn enough, devoted enough to power, there remains this last apocalyptic myth of machinery propagating its own kind in the eschatological wilderness of space—while on earth the bombs make room!

But the others: they remain imprisoned in other hopes, and in more pedestrian despairs, despairs and hopes which are held down to earth, down to street level, and to the pavement only: desire to be at least half-human, to taste a little human joy, to do a fairly decent job of productive work, to come home to the family . . . desires for which there is no room. It is in these that He hides Himself, for whom there is no room.

The time of the end? All right: when?

That is not the question.

To say it is the time of the end is to answer all the questions, for if it is the time of the end, and of great tribulation, then it is certainly and above all the time of The Great Joy. It is the time to "lift up your heads for your redemption is at hand." It is the time when the promise will be manifestly fulfilled, and no longer kept secret from anyone. It is the time for the joy that is given not as the world gives, and that no man can take away.

For the true eschatological banquet is not that of the birds on the bodies of the slain. It is the feast of the living, the wedding banquet of the Lamb. The true eschatological convocation is not the crowding of armies on the field of battle, but the summons of The Great Joy, the cry of deliverance: "Come out of her my people that you may not share in her sins and suffer from her plagues!" (Revelations 18:4). The cry of the time of the end was uttered also in the beginning by Lot in Sodom, to his sons-in-law: "Come, get out of this city, for the Lord will destroy it. But he seemed to them to be jesting" (Genesis 19:14).

To leave the city of death and imprisonment is surely not bad news except to those who have so identified themselves with their captivity that they can conceive no other reality and no other condition. In such a case, there is nothing but tribulation: for while to stay in captivity is tragic, to break away from it is unthinkable —and so more tragic still.

What is needed then is the grace and courage to see that "The Great Tribulation" and "The Great Joy" are really inseparable, and that the "Tribulation" becomes "Joy" when it is seen as the Victory of Life over Death.

True, there is a sense in which there is no room for Joy in this tribulation. To say there is "no room" for The Great Joy in the tribulation of "the end" is to say that the Evangelical joy must not be confused with the joys proposed by the world in the time of the end—and, we must admit it, these are no longer convincing as joys. They become now stoic duties and sacrifices to be offered without question for ends that cannot be descried just now, since there is too much smoke and the visibility is rather poor. In the last analysis, the "joy" proposed by the time of the end is simply the satisfaction and the relief of getting it all over with . . .

That is the demonic temptation of "the end." For eschatology is not *finis* and punishment, the winding up of accounts and the closing of books: it is the final beginning, the definitive birth into a new creation. It is not the last gasp of exhausted possibilities but the first taste of all that is beyond conceiving as actual.

But can we believe it? ("He seemed to them to be jesting!")

75

Prometheus: A Meditation

PREFATORY NOTE: TWO FACES OF PROMETHEUS

ERASMUS once discussed with Colet and other divines the nature of Cain's sin: not the murder of Abel but his *first* sin. Their conclusions are no longer interesting. The only reason I allude to the discussion is that the Cain of Erasmus turned out to be Prometheus in a fable that tells us much about the mentality of the Renaissance—and about our own.

Cain, says Erasmus, had often heard his parents speak of the wonderful vegetation of Paradise, where the "ears of corn were as high as the alders," and he persuaded the angel at the gate to bring him a few seeds from inside the garden. He planted them and succeeded admirably as a farmer, but this drew down upon him the wrath of the Almighty. His sacrifices were no longer acceptable.

It is curiously significant that modern man should consider himself somehow called upon to vindicate Cain, and that in doing so he should identify Cain with the fire-bearing Titan whom he has been pleased to make the symbol of his own technological genius and of his cosmic aspirations.

But what is equally significant is the confusion of the two opposite interpretations of Prometheus: the version of Hesiod, in which Prometheus is a villain, and the version of Aeschylus in which he is the hero. The difference between these two versions lies of course in the different attitude toward the implacable father figure: Zeus.

Hesiod represents and approves the Olympian order, where Zeus reigns in absolute power over the subversive and dethroned gods of archaic Greece. Zeus is the god of the invading Achaians who destroyed the matriarchal and tribal society of primitive Greece, the world of the Earth Mother, of Demeter and of Hera. Prometheus, the son of Earth and of Ocean, is a threat to the static order established by Zeus, the order in which no bird may chirp and no flower may look at the sun without the permission of the jealous Father. Zeus is the master of life rather than its giver. He tolerates man and man's world, but only barely.

According to Hesiod, when Prometheus *stole* the fire for men (there was no other way in which he could get fire away from Zeus) Zeus revenged himself on Prometheus in the way we well know, with the added detail that he drives a stake through his heart. But Zeus is also revenged upon mankind: how? By sending woman.

Strange, ponderous fantasy of an aggressively male society! Woman comes from Zeus as a *punishment,* for in her "everything is good but her heart."

80

Woman, the culminating penance in a life of labor and sorrow!

In the world picture of Hesiod, though it is beautiful, primitive, full of Hellenic clarity, we find this darkness, this oppressive and guilty view that life and love are somehow a punishment. That nothing can ever be really good in it. That life is slavery and sorrow because of Zeus, and because Prometheus has resisted Zeus. That therefore life is nothing but a wheel upon which man is broken like a slave. . . .

Epimetheus, the brother of Prometheus, receives woman as a gift from Zeus and does not wake up to the nature of the gift until it is too late. Then he remembers what Prometheus had told him: *never accept any gift from the gods.*

Hesiod is a great poet and yet this view of life is cold, negative and odious. In any case I hate it— All the more because it is, I believe, implicit in the atheism of the world into which I was born and out of which, by Christ's grace and the gift of God, I have been reborn.

The *Prometheus Bound* of Aeschylus is one of the purest and most sacred of tragedies. I know of none that strikes so deep into the roots of man, the root where man is able to live in the mystery of God.

The Prometheus of Aeschylus is the exact opposite of the Prometheus of Hesiod. Between Prometheus and the Earth Mother and Ocean rises the figure of a usurper. For in Aeschylus it is Zeus, not Prometheus, who is the usurper. It is Zeus, not Prometheus, who is sick with *hubris*. True, Prometheus is driven by desperation beyond the wise limits which the Greek mind recognized so well. But his rebellion is the rebellion of life against inertia and death, of mercy and love against tyranny, of humanity against cruelty and arbitrary violence. And he calls upon the feminine, the wordless, the timelessly moving elements to witness his sufferings. Earth hears him.

In the end of the tragedy (which is only the first of a trilogy, two plays of which have been lost) Earth promises her son a deliverer. Herakles will come and break his brother's chains. Zeus will be mollified. His mind will change, and he will see things in a new light. The struggling gods will be reconciled, and the reconciliation will be the victory of Prometheus but also the victory of Earth, that is to say of mercy, of humanity, of innocence, of trust.

Once more it will be possible for men to receive gifts from heaven. It will be possible and right to wait for gifts, to depend on them. To use them to build, innocently, a better world.

The two faces of Prometheus represent two attitudes toward life, one positive, the other negative. It is significant that the Renaissance, in choosing between the two, selected the negative. It is against this negative choice that my Prometheus is written. My meditation is a rejection of the negative, modern myth of Prometheus. It is a return to the archaic, Aeschylean and positive aspect of Prometheus, which is, at the same time, to my mind, deeply and implicitly Christian.

The Prometheus of Hesiod is Cain. The Prometheus of Aeschylus is Christ on the Cross.

In my meditation I have started from Hesiod's view in order to argue against it.

PROMETHEUS: A MEDITATION

1. The small gods men have made for themselves are jealous fathers, only a little greater than their sons, only a little stronger, only a little wiser. Immortal fathers, afraid of their mortal children, they are unjustly protected by a too fortunate immortality. To fight with them requires at once heroism and despair. The man who does not know the Living God is condemned, by his own gods, to this despair: because, knowing that he has made his own gods, he cannot help hoping that he will be able to overthrow them. Alas, he realizes too late that he has made them immortal. They must eventually devour him.

2. The Promethean instinct is as deep as man's weakness: that is to say, it is almost infinite. Promethean despair is the cry that rises out of the abyss of man's

nothingness—the inarticulate expression of the terror man cannot face, the terror of having to be someone, of having to be himself. That is to say, his terror of facing and fully realizing his divine sonship, in Christ, and in the Spirit of Fire Who is given us from heaven. The fire Prometheus thought he had to steal from the gods is his own identity in God, the affirmation and vindication of his own being as a sanctified creature in the image of God. The fire Prometheus thought he had to steal was his own spiritual freedom. In the eyes of Prometheus, to be himself was to be guilty. The exercise of liberty was a crime, an attack upon the gods which he had made (the gods to whom he had given all that was good in himself, so that in order to have all that he had, it was necessary to steal it back from them).

3. Prometheus knows—for his nature tells him this—that he must become a person. Yet he feels that he can only do this by an exploit, a *tour-de-force*. And the exploit itself is doomed to failure. Condemned by his very nature to this gesture and this crime, he feels drawn, by his very nature itself, to extinction. The fire attracts him more than he can believe possible, because it is in reality his own. But he hates himself for desiring what he has given to his gods, and punishes himself before he can take it back from them. Then he becomes his own vulture, and is satisfied at last. In consuming himself, he finds realization. (Secretly he tells himself: "I

84

have won fire for other men, I have sacrified myself for others." But in reality he has won nothing for anybody. He has suffered the loss of his own soul, but he has not gained the whole world, or even a small part of it. He has gained nothing.)

4. Guilty, frustrated, rebellious, fear-ridden, Prometheus seeks to assert himself and fails. His mysticism enables him to glory in defeat. For since Prometheus cannot conceive of a true victory, his own triumph is to let the vulture devour his liver: he will be a martyr and a victim, because the gods he has created in his own image represent his own tyrannical demands upon himself. There is only one issue in his struggle with them: glorious defiance in a luxury of despair.

To struggle with the gods seems great indeed to those who do not know the Living God. They do not know that He is on our side against false gods, and defeat is not permissible. One who loves Christ is not allowed to be Prometheus. He is not allowed to fail. He must *keep* the fire that is given him from heaven. And he must assert that the fire is *his*. He must maintain his rights against all the false gods who hold that it was stolen.

5. Guilt was the precious gift of the false gods to Prometheus, a gift that made all this waste possible. Not knowing that the fire was his for the asking, a gift of the true God, the Living God, not knowing that fire was

something God did not need for Himself (since He had made it expressly for man) Prometheus felt he was obliged to steal what he could not do without. And why? Because he knew no god that would be willing to give it to him for nothing. He could not conceive of such a god, because if he himself had been god, he would have needed fire for himself and would never have shared it with another. He knew no god that was not an enemy, because the gods he knew were only a little stronger than himself, and needed fire as badly as he needed it. In order to exist at all, they had to dominate him, feed on him and ruin him (for if he himself had been a god, he knew he would have had to live on what was weaker than himself).

Thus the gods Prometheus knew were weak, because he himself was weak. Yet they were a little stronger than he was, strong enough to chain him to Caucasus. (He had that much strength left in himself, after creating his gods: he was strong enough to consume himself for all eternity in punishment for having desired their fire. In fact, he destroyed himself forever that they might live. For this reason idolatry was, and is, the fundamental sin.)

6.   A man must make the best of whatever gods he has. Prometheus had to have weak gods because he was his own god, and no man admits that he is his own god. But he subjects himself to his own weakness, conceived as a

god, and prefers it to the strength of the Living God. If Prometheus had known the strong God, and not worshiped weak gods, things would have been different. The guilt Prometheus felt from the beginning was more necessary for his gods than for himself. If he had not been guilty, such gods would not have been able to exist. Without guilt he could not have conceived them, and since they only existed in his own mind he had to be guilty in order to think of them at all. His guilt, then, was a secret expression of love. It was his homage of love and trust. By his guilt he bore witness to his little household gods, his fire-hoarders. By stealing their fire he confessed that he loved them and believed in their falsity more than he loved the Living God and more than he believed in His truth. It was then a supreme act of homage on his part to open his heart to his unreal gods, and steal from them that fire which, in reality, was his own. Surely, he had given them everything, in order to show how much he preferred their nothingness to the Living God and even to himself!

7. No one was ever less like Prometheus on Caucasus than Christ on His Cross. For Prometheus thought he had to ascend into heaven to steal what God had already decreed to give him. But Christ, Who had in Himself all the riches of God and all the poverty of Prometheus, came down with the fire Prometheus needed, hidden in His Heart. And He had Himself put to death next to

the thief Prometheus in order to show him that in reality God cannot seek to keep anything good to Himself alone.

Far from killing the man who seeks the divine fire, the Living God will Himself pass through death in order that man may have what is destined for him.

If Christ has died and risen from the dead and poured out upon us the fire of His Holy Spirit, why do we imagine that our desire for life is a Promethean desire, doomed to punishment?

Why do we act as if our longing to "see good days" were something God did not desire, when He Himself told us to seek them?

Why do we reproach ourselves for desiring victory? Why do we pride ourselves on our defeats, and glory in despair?

Because we think our life is important to ourselves alone, and do not know that our life is more important to the Living God than it is to our own selves.

Because we think our happiness is for ourselves alone, and do not realize that it is also His happiness.

Because we think our sorrows are for ourselves alone, and do not believe that they are much more than that: they are His sorrows.

There is nothing we can steal from Him at all, because before we can think of stealing it, it has already been given.

Atlas and the Fatman

ON the last day of a rough but fortunate voyage, near the farthest end of the known world, I found my way to the shores of a sentient mountain.

There stood the high African rock in the shadow of lucky rain: a serious black crag, at the tip of the land mass, with a cloud balanced on its shoulder.

O high silent man of lava, with feet in the green surf, watching the stream of days and years!

We saw the clouds drift by the face of that tame god, and held our peace. We placed our feet on the hot sands as the ship ran aground on the edge of night and of summer.

This was Atlas at his lonely work! I never thought I would have seen his face!

His head was hidden in cloud and night. His eyes were staring darkness. His thoughts were full of inscrutable waters. His heart was safe at the bottom of the green ocean. His spirit stood silent and awake in the center of the world.

He held everything in massive silence. In one deep thought without words he kept the continents from drifting apart. The seas obeyed not his eyes, not his words, but the beating of his heart.

His only utterance was one weak light in a lighthouse. Small sharp words, no commentary on the pure mystery of night, they left the mystery alone: touched it and left it alone.

From time to time he spoke (but only to the distance) with the short bass clangor of a bell. The neutral note was uttered, and said nothing.

Yet it was this dim bell in the heavens that moved the weather and changed the seasons. A new summer grew upon the ocean, before our eyes, closely followed by autumn, then winter.

The waves moved by with white hair. Time rode the secret waves, commanded only by Atlas and by his bell. There were ages passing by as we watched. Birds skimmed the white-haired ages. Young birds kept the morning young. The silence of this unvisited shore embraced the beginning of history and its end.

We made believe that it was five o'clock. We made believe that it was six o'clock. We made believe that it was midnight. Atlas must have deigned to smile on our efforts, since it was now dark. His eyes gave hope to the tumbling ocean. Once again, rain began to fall.

When it is evening, when night begins to darken, when rain is warm in the summer darkness and rumors come up from the woods and from the banks of rivers, then shores and forests sound around you with a wordless solicitude of mothers. It is then that flowering palms enchant the night with their sweet smell. Flowers sleep. Thoughts become simple. Words cease. The hollows of the mind fill with dreams as with water.

In the sacred moment between sleep and staying awake, Atlas speaks to the night as to a woman. He speaks freely to the night he loves, thinking no one is at hand.

He speaks of his heart at the bottom of the ocean. He speaks of his spirit at the center of the world. He speaks of fires that night and woman do not understand. Green fires that are extinguished by intelligence, that night and woman possess. Golden fires of spirit that are in the damp warm rocky roots of the earth. White fires that are clear outside of earth and sky which night and woman cannot reach. And waters that are common to night and to woman and to Atlas, ruled by a bell in the moon and by a bell in the sun.

Atlas puts out all those fires with his one bell, and looks at nothing. This is the work that supports the activity of seasons: Atlas looking at nothing.

"How lonely is my life as a mountain on the shore of ocean with my heart at the bottom of the sea and my spirit at the center of the earth where no one can speak to me. I ring my bell and nobody listens. All I do is look at nothing and change the seasons and hold up the sky and save the world.

"No one will come near to one so tall, no one will befriend one so strong as I, and I am forgotten forever. It is right that I be forgotten, for if I were not forgotten where would be my vigilance, and if I were not vigilant where would be the world? And if night and woman could understand my thoughts, where would be my strength? My thoughts would draw up my spirit from the center of the earth and the whole world would fall into emptiness.

"My stability is without fault because I have no connections. I have not viewed mankind for ages. Yet I have not slept, thinking of man and his troubles, which are not alleviated by the change of seasons. I wish well to mankind. I give man more seasons and pray that he be not left to himself. I want him not to see my far lights upon the ocean (this is impossible) or hear my dim bell in the heavens (this is not expedient). But I want him to rest at peace under a safe sky knowing that I am here with my lights and my bell and that the ends of the world are watched by an overseer and the seas taken care of.

"I do not tire easily, for this is the work I am used to. Though it is child's play, sometimes I hate it. I bear with loneliness for the sake of man. Yet to be constantly forgotten is more than I can abide.

"Thus I intend not only to watch, but to move watching, and I shall begin by moving the theaters."

At this there was a stir in all the distant cities of the world and the continents heaved up and down like the trays of a scale, as all the great countries were suddenly weighed by Atlas in the middle of the night: the lands of Europe and the lands of Asia were weighed in the hands of a tall hidden power, and knew nothing of it. The shores of America waited in the mist to be weighed in the same balance. It was Atlas, the guardian of nights and seas moving and watching.

We expected movement only after it had already begun and we looked for power when the strong were already overthrown. We saw the dance begin secretly in genteel houses, under the kitchen oilcloth, and leap to the tops of the most public monuments. Some buildings woke and walked downhill and would not stop until they came to water. Churches and banks begged pardon as they slipped and fell. People in the unsafe doors set out for earth that escaped them, and trod too late on streets that hurried away. It was more than most men could afford but far more than they could avoid. It was a lame evening. No taxi would take any man to the right place.

This was what happened everywhere when the movement began. The title of the earthquake was "Atlas watches every evening."

Then up jumped a great Fatman in one of the stadiums. He thought that he was god and that he could stop everything from moving. He thought that since he could, he had to. He cried out loud. He swore at the top of his voice. He fired off a gun and made the people listen. He roared and he boasted and made himself known. He blew back into the wind and stamped on the rolling earth and swore up and down he could make it all stop with his invention. He got up in the teeth of the storm and made a loud speech which everybody heard. And the first thing he said was this:

"If anything moves, I am the one to move it: and if anything stops, I am the one to stop it. If anything shakes, I am the one to shake it, and not one being is going to budge unless pushed."

At that moment everything stopped. No one had heard the dim bell at the edge of the sea (which Atlas had struck, in his dream, at this very moment). No one saw the lights in the dark at the edge of the ocean (which had gone on and off with a passing memory in that far place). No one thought of anything, the Fatman had all their attention.

Now this Fatman had been brought up on oats and meat and his name was secret. His father was a grocer and his mother was a butcher. His father was a tailor and his mother ran a train. His father was a brewer and his mother was a general in the army. He had been born with leather hands and a clockwork mind in order to make a lot of money. He hated the country and loved stadiums: a perfect, civilized man! His number was six hundred and sixty-six and he worked hard building up the stadium Atlas had destroyed.

All the people brought him money and played music to him because he was rich. And the music was so loud no one heard the bell ring again. Once again the houses began to tremble.

No one looked at anything, but fixed their eyes only on the Fatman in his rage. No one heard Atlas far off thinking in the smoke. All they knew was that the city began to fall again and the Fatman roared in the tumbledown theaters: "If I had my way there would be RAIN." He held up his hands and had his way. Rain came down as sudden as a black mountain. The clock struck ten. The world stopped moving. Everyone attributed this to the Fatman whose name was secret.

Then in the holes of the broken city the sergeants smiled safe and guns became a thing of the present. Gas was mercy then to many a Jew mother and a quick end came to more than a few as a gift of the popular state. "Here comes a chemical death, with the smile of the public Father. You shall be cheaply made extinct as a present from economy, and we will save your hair and teeth. Cyanide hopes are the face of a popular tomorrow, with ever more fun in the underwears. Everybody has dollars in the home of well-run Demos, and more for cars than for Sunday. But Sunday is public also where Fatman has his office. Only a different name, that's all.

"Here comes chemical Sunday, with a smile of the Fatman's ghost father. They take the girth of the Fat

Father's own gas, on top of the ancient marsh, in the name of a new culture. Toy thugs jump out of every cradle with weapons in their hands. They swing by hard and mean in the name of popularity and boy, that popularity is going to make you jump. It is already famous what they can do with guns, and more so with a piece of small invented pipe, all for the fame and benefit of the new police. Fatman, Fatman, blow us a gassy kiss from the four chimneys of your new heaven!"

From the four sides of the wind there came together in trolleys a set of delegations in the name of Dad. "Not forgetting Mom," they blowed, "we come to hail the Fatman in the name of Dad." And old Dad sat up high in the memories of the police, a nineteenth-century legend, a corncob angle measuring the west. A piece of trueblue oldgold faked-up fortune. True Dad is all fixed up in the mind like a piece of Real Estate, but Mom (cries the Fatman) Mom is real heart and all soft in the easies. Mom is fat from toe to toe, and slimmer than an ankle. Good old American Maw is Father's boast on wedding-cake afternoon, in the days of Coca-Cola. Maw is safe in the new car and Paw cares for corners. The eyes of the innocent sergeant salute Maw with pride as they draw Negro blood. And we will have a clean America for our boys, clean as the toy toughs punished in rugged Lux. Tomboy Maw is the magic of Fatman's perpetual boast.

Then the Fatman, moved by intuition, placed his feet in the water and established contact with the spirit of night, and the waves thrashed about his knees. All at once he began to grow. He gave up meat to become an ascetic. He drank only the most inexpensive mouthwash. He dealt with woman only by mail. He tried out his hands on the sky and began to hold up the firmament. He would hold up the sky and preach at the same time, for he was suddenly religious. He began to list all the dates of history and to tell men another word for love and another word for death. He said he himself was the eldest child of love and death, but principally of death. At this he returned to his meat and dropped his letters and dealt with woman once again directly. He said he could also tell them another name for woman. The people took down notes of what he said next, and he told them his own real name was god.

We who stood far off amid the tears of the African night, we who stood with our feet on a hot land, we knew who had rung the bell and changed the weather. We knew who had sent rain. We knew which was power and which was image, which was light and which was legend. And we knew which of the two had his heart at the bottom of the ocean. We knew who watched and who moved under the theaters every time the bell rang. We listened intently to the cloud and the darkness. We lived upon distance, and leaned upon emptiness until we heard our mountain think plain in his own cloud.

"Smoke is not measured by clocks," said Atlas. "Time is not told by disasters. Years are not numbered by the wars that are in them, days are not marked on the calendar for the murders that take place on them. What is it that you are measuring, Fatman? What is it that you are interpreting with your machine, meatman? What is it that you are counting, you square, serious stepson of death?

"I take my own time," said Atlas, "which is the time of the sea. The sea tells it own long time, not by the moon or by the sun or by any clock. The time of the sea is infinitely various, and out of it comes all life: but only when the time of the sea is the time of the sun. Not the time of rising and setting, but the time of light itself, which has no hours.

"The sea's time is the time of long life. The jungle's time is the time of many rains. The spirit of the trees takes up time out of the slow earth and the leaves are made of this earthtime turning into light. Longer life still undersea, for invisible Tritons. The long life of the earth. The life of spinning suns.

"The gods of the sea tell no time. They are busy with their own music. I, Atlas, improve the world with mists, evenings and colors. I have my own music of clouds, skies and centuries. I strike music from far continents. Others do not hear. They have heard nothing of this for a long time. They have heard clock and cannon, not my music. They have eaten smoke and gone down by train to the last mute home of welfare, which is the end.

"Sad is the city of the Fatman, for all his industry. Snow cannot make softer the city of the Fatman, which is always black in its own breath. Rain cannot wash clean the city of the mercenary, which is always gray with his own despair. Light cannot make fair their houses or wine their faces, though they swim in millions they have won. The Fatman with his inventions is propping up a fallen heaven."

Shall we forget the periods of his earthly mischief, not with regret? Shall we forget the Fatman and his false rain? The people in that city shuddered and the rain ran down their necks and the Fatman struggled with his stadium.

"Fatman," said Atlas, "you are a faithless mad son of clocks and buzzers. I do not know what apparatus was your sire, you bastard of two machines, born with another million. Your mother is not the ocean, your father has not the sun in his heart, you do not know the smell of the earth, your blood is not your own; it is taken from armies. A red flash goes on and off for every thought in your head and a buzzer announces your latest word. I abhor the traffic that comes from such a mad, convulsive mouth. It is the mouth of a horde, the mouth of a system, the mouth of a garage, the mouth of a commission."

Atlas stopped speaking and the rain ended. The Fatman raged in his place and all the people sweated under attack. Crowds expected the Fatman to stand up for his honor and for the first time to move the world with his invention. Instead he only argued with himself and though he bragged he instantly called himself a liar. But in the same breath he accused Atlas of the most shameful infamies. "Atlas is responsible," he said, "for doors and windows, stairs, chimneys, and every other form of evil." In attacking Atlas he ended by moving no one but himself, and this was the burden of his display:

"Thirteen is an unlucky number and there are *thirteen in this theater.*" (This was his first bravery and very nearly his last, the heart of his argument. For though he said much more, he barely moved beyond this point: oh lucky thirteen!)

"Do you see," he cried, "do you see around me the thirteen beards of Victor Hugo and Karl Marx? Do you see around me the spectacles of Edison, Rockefeller, and behind me the comforting pokerfaces of Stakhanov and Patton? Do you see above my head the thirteen mustaches of Hitler and of Stalin? You who see these thirteen see me and my fathers. . . .

"Now I have fought the elements for thirteen days and nights with my invention. The elements will never be the same again. There were thirteen floods when the world was destroyed for the first time and thirteen sat together at supper in one room when very big business was done by my cousin Judas. (My cousins all prosper in business. We are not lucky in love.)

"Now that the fates are measuring more fires for the cities of men, and I myself am inventing more of them, and walls begin to shake at the work of the atheist Atlas, I stand here to defy walls, fires, earthquake and enemy. I stand here to defy Atlas. Yes I stand here in the name of clean government to defy this upsquirt downpush four-five-six confusion of aliens. Yes I maintain this Atlas is no longer public, and never was mechanical. Is he insured? Has he a license? Ask him for his card, his thumbprint, and his serial number. Has he been registered? Has he been certified? I have been all these things not once but thirteen times, which is fourteen stars on my best stripe. I am the auspicious beginning and the prosperous end, the lucky winner and the marvelous defeat. I am alone in the public eye on thirteen counts. Mine is the middle of the stadium.

"I alone shall shake walls in the future. I alone shall light thirteen fires. I alone shall determine right and wrong; establish time and season; plan day and night as I please, and the sex and the future of children. I alone shall spite or command sea, wind and element. And now by God I hear thirteen allegedly just men walking under the oilcloth and if they don't stop I'LL FIRE!"

Well, as you might expect, the citizens came out with bands to hail the Fatman, since this had been arranged. But the Fatman by now was lost in his own smoke. The strength ebbed out of his invention, and his hands fell slack; his eyes popped out and his fat began to get away from him in all the heat he had caused with his speech. The men in the bands continued to perspire and blow. Their horns would shiver till the drums fell in. There was no rain and the Fatman was smaller than a baby. Winds were still as death; buildings swayed for the last fall. Everyone knew the Fatman would not get out of the way in time. Generals cried to the Fatman as they left by all windows, telling him to jump, but nobody heard his answer.

Then Atlas stood over the world holding up the sky like a great wall of clear ice and the Fatman saw Atlas was not his friend. The Fatman was blinded by the glare of the ice and closed his eyes upon a world that had been made hateful by his own folly.

So winter comes to the ocean and the quiet city wears plumes of smoke upon helmets of ice. It is a time of golden windows and of a steel sun, a time of more bitter cruelty than before, though the Fatman is gone. For even the just man now kills without compunction, because it is duty to be hard and to destroy is mercy. Justice is a myth made of numbers. Mercy is love of system. Christmas goes by without a sound because there are no sinners anymore, everyone is just.

No need of feast days when everyone is just: no one needs to be saved. No one needs to think. No one needs to confess.

The cold saints of the new age count with their machine the bitter, methodical sacrifices they are making in the Fatman's memory, and stand in line before his tomb. Sacrifice is counted in drops of blood (where blood is still left, for many can do without it).

Minutes are counted like Aztecs walking a man to his death with his heart out on top of a bad pyramid: such is order and justice. Such is the beauty of system.

So the children of scandal sit all day in the icy windows and try in vain to shed one tear: but in a time of justice tears are of no avail.

For the just man there is no consolation.

For the good there is no pardon.

For the holy there is no absolution.

Let no man speak of anything but Law, and let no work support anyone but the police.

These are the saints the Fatman has left us in the kingdom of his order. . . .

Yet Tritons under the sea must once again move.

When warmth comes again to the sea the Tritons of spring shall wake. Life shall wake underground and under sea. The fields will laugh, the woods will be drunk with flowers of rebellion, the night will make every fool sing in his sleep, and the morning will make him stand up in the sun and cover himself with water and with light.

There is another kind of justice than the justice of number, which can neither forgive nor be forgiven. There is another kind of mercy than the mercy of Law which knows no absolution. There is a justice of new-born worlds which cannot be counted. There is a mercy of individual things that spring into being without reason. They are just without reason, and their mercy is without explanation. They have received rewards beyond description because they themselves refuse to be described. They are virtuous in the sight of God because their names do not identify them. Every plant that stands in the light of the sun is a saint and an outlaw. Every tree that brings forth blossoms without the command of man is powerful in the sight of God. Every star that man has not counted is a world of sanity and perfection. Every blade of grass is an angel singing in a shower of glory.

These are worlds of themselves. No man can use or destroy them. Theirs is the life that moves without being seen and cannot be understood. It is useless to look for what is everywhere. It is hopeless to hope for what cannot be gained because you already have it. The fire of a wild white sun has eaten up the distance between hope and despair. Dance in this sun, you tepid idiot. Wake up and dance in the clarity of perfect contradiction.

You fool, it is life that makes you dance: have you forgotten? Come out of the smoke, the world is tossing in its sleep, the sun is up, the land is bursting in the silence of dawn. The clear bell of Atlas rings once again over the sea and the animals come to the shore at his feet. The gentle earth relaxes and spreads out to embrace the strong sun. The grasses and flowers speak their own secret names. With his great gentle hands, Atlas opens the clouds and birds spill back onto the land out of Paradise.

You fool, the prisons are open. The Fatman is forgotten. The Fatman was only his own nightmare. Atlas never knew him. Atlas never knew anything but the ways of the stars, of the earth and of the ocean. Atlas is a friendly mountain, with a cloud on his shoulder, watching the African sun.

Martin's Predicament
or Atlas Watches
Every Evening

NOTE: This is another, earlier treatment of the Atlas myth, less developed and less poetic. The themes of creativity, power, destruction and facticity are again evident—but the tone is intentionally trifling. These lines may be read as notes for a puppet show. It is nothing more.

I

Martin said "every sane man" would hesitate to believe what we were now about to see. For seeing is imagining. Imagining is make-believe. Who can make anyone believe that Atlas watches? Yet it is true; he watches every evening.

Watches what? This was to become Martin's big question.

II

The scene is a large gray yard with a view of the Atlantic. The waters clash, as in a dream. The ocean is before you with a boat and a bell and a cloud and a lighthouse. Look! It all moves!

Watch the tumbling shapes everywhere. The seas

change their minds. Time goes past with white hair—
Time's winged chariot which always goes too far.
Time comes up from very far and keeps on coming. Be
a witness!

Now make believe it is five o'clock; now make believe
it is six o'clock; now make believe it is seven.

(We hear the great hollow pianos of the Atlantic. In
the evening the waters address us with mindless solicitude, like that of programs.)

III

Wave after wave. Cloud upon cloud. Silence after
silence. Shapes come in by every exit and go out by the
door in the roof. Our roof opens into the sky. The
clouds know the way. East and West. Time flies, and
Atlas watches.

IV

Martin, John, and Eva come by different doors into
the room. There are chairs, a sofa, and a huge fireplace.
There is a picture of Victor Hugo. Soon the four of
them are alone with a piano. I shall never forget this
afternoon: the snow that falls, the cards that are not
played, the subtle movements of aggression that lead
to every new phase in the conversation.

—Can't you stay still a minute? I want to take a
photograph.

—Are you right to say such things about Father?

—Father would smile if he could hear you speaking now!

—But would we speak, unless Father were smiling?

Martin sits in the central chair and produces many tentative names for the personage who is the subject of their conversation: Father Mussorgsky; Father Van Tellen; Father Ed Coogan; Father Joy; Father Blue; Father Post; Father Grogan.

"Why," laughs Eva merrily, "I don't believe we even *have* a Father."

Here is a burst of sudden humor that dispels every cloud, so Martin sits down at the piano. Music goes on for a long time. A merry evening.

Long live the Queen!

Long live civilization!

V

Eva opens and reads aloud two letters she has received from Atlas:

"Far from my loved ones I eke out a laborious and distracted existence. Does anyone give me a thought? Does anyone recognize himself indebted to my care for the common comfort and security of the human race?"

And:

"Since I have been so completely forgotten I feel that it is time for me to move watching. Hitherto I have watched. Now I shall also move. I shall be called,

"Moves Watching." I intend to begin with the theaters. I shall move all the theaters. I shall not betray your expectation. I shall begin tomorrow evening.

Eva looks significantly at the others who exclaim in unison: "At this very moment we are sitting in a theater."

It was already tomorrow evening.

VI

—I am concerned only with rewards and exiles.

—That explains your remorse.

—You touch me deeply. What did the girls say?

—Remember it has only happened once, but once is enough. If it has to happen more often, nobody will know what to think. But it did happen at least once, and for once all were ready with an explanation. In spite of a moment of doubt, reason surrendered and the whole thing was explained in terminology.

—There were lots of photographs; one would have been sufficient.

—Such luxuries are no longer expensive.

—But they will reassure Father and Mother.

—That is what the bells said.

—Good-by. See you in the mirror! (Ah! Civilization!)

VII

"If we were going to play a spelling game," says Eva, "we could spell things like 'civilization is hanging in the balance if not on the gallows.' But this is not the time for jesting since the movement we were expecting has already begun!"

In fact the earth has secretly moved. The carpets have stirred unnoticed under the feet of the visitors and the portrait of Victor Hugo has turned its face to the wall. Soon everybody will surprise everybody else in a meeting on all the roads out of town. Something is closing in upon human nature that is more than most men can afford, but it is too general to be avoided. They suffer the very insecurities they least expected. Their feet will not carry them to the right taxi and all the machinery is going backwards.

Then Eva knows by experience that Atlas moves watching, and that watching is moving without seeing —except to see that it is all moving.

"An odd philosophy," she thinks, as the wall parts in front of her, "But we must make the best of it now!"

VIII

Then Martin bravely dictates a telegram to Atlas in which he makes known all his qualifications for the new office of world-moderator. "For," he declares, "these movements must not be left to mere instinct." He is encouraged by Eva to "explain everything." He writes:

"I never had to exert myself in gymnasiums. Both strength and skill came naturally. I was majestic in the cradle, and knew it well. At the age of two I was able to cut my own hair but didn't as my parents were rich and we had many servants. When I was six I taught Greek in a small but decent college.

(Oh the perverse dignities of scholarship, thinks Eva aloud, over his shoulder.)

"In the most elegant houses I grew up out of the rain and had no holes in my stockings. I kept all the rain out of my room and out of my clothing. I was perfect in deportment. I kept my friends and entertainers dry at all times in my limousines. I protected all because I was myself protected by all. Who could worry for a moment about the future? I grew up in the most distinguished vehicles. I grew up dry in the most expensive torrents of rain. I was hard to meet, of course, and seldom seen: rarely even in pictures. But imagine my strength! Imagine my hunger! Imagine my insatiable need for love! Imagine my demand for more than my own fair share of parents!

"Meanwhile I migrated from the scenic wonders and honeymoon cathedrals of antique overseas and settled in a fast-moving new continent where I developed a unique voice, the voice of the friend. I became a warmly trusted consultant of adult women and was kept so busy I developed bad eating habits. Yet I still loved pets. I became a seasoned traveler with an unpredictable schedule. I was connoisseur of versatile mixtures and occult taste-bud formularies, not to mention medicines! I was air-conditioned from stem to stern, a smooth sport, loving the surge of power under the pedal. I sent the no-risk reply-card to the jolly meat packers and re-read my own complete plays as an introductory gift. I married two eligible prospects simultaneously and we three walked hand in hand into the glorious but uncertain future.

"How can I avoid making friends when I need them so badly and am, in fact, almost never my own friend? I am so rich that I can buy up all their loneliness at once. All their solitudes are mine. I support them without being supported. I am alone. I am alone in the midst of those who love me. Now they are about to fall head-long into the hole. Can I prevent them? I must seek out the acquaintance of a man of power. Yet I myself am the only man of power.

"It is clear that with my immense wealth I can support Atlas, and thereby the whole grateful world. This is the rich song I have composed for the occasion:

> By myself
> in large numbers,
> all together
> by myself.
> Growing daily richer
> I'm a population
> by myself.
> I'm a one-man city
> by myself.

117

This new song takes in the whole question of being so rich that you can supersede everybody else. I don't think that isn't pretty good."

No one can put into words the unspoken question: "Will Atlas answer? Can he even read this kind of language?"

IX

While they are waiting Eva smiles and says: "Victor Hugo has reserved for you a pleasant surprise: When the buildings moved he swam the ocean, and now he is *here!*"

—Well! He ought to go to confession!

As a matter of fact, the Great French Poet is now smiling in his beard.

X

"Do not be deceived," says Martin, who has worried silently for a long time: "if it moves it is mine. I am the one to tell it when to tick and when to sit still. We have seen that there was nobody watching in the ocean and there is no consciousness in the sky. Atlas has refused to answer letters. He cannot account for the present mood of exasperation. We have explored his presumed locality and found nothing. He has not moved on this or any other evening. If the movement seems to continue, as it unfortunately does, we must have a plan:

my plan. We must have imperatives. And in fact we have them. I may humbly say that I am a man of imperatives. I am jokingly referred to as "Mr. Imperative." He stands up and begins to dictate telegrams: *Plan complete protection and worldwide total control remaining flexible while matching research with cosmic needs NOW! With treble and quadruple resources and split-second selection of non-motivated objectives we will upgrade dramatic DECISIONS and ACT GLOBALLY.*

We will not shrink from self-contradiction this or any other season, but we will implement a wide-open policy of antic dislocation focusing on round-the-clock professional carefree extermination programs. I proclaim this gala club opportunity and invite you to join me NOW!

XI

Eva picks up the telephone and dials Atlas but there is no answer.

Another wall collapses.

XII

Now it is John's turn.

"Smoke is not measured by minutes," he says quietly. "The sea tells its own long time, and not by the moon nor by any clock is the sea's time told. The sea's time is the time of a long life. The long life undersea of great invisible Tritons. The gods of the sea tell no time, busy themselves with their own music. It is a music of mist and waves and clouds. It is a music of centuries. I have not heard any of this for a long time. I have heard the bells and the clocks but I have not heard this music. Martin, you are a faithless mad son of clocks and bells. I do not know who is your father, but your mother is not the ocean, and your father has not had the ocean in his heart; his heart has been possessed by clock and computer. A bell rings for every thought in his head and a light goes on for his approaching words. I avoid the traffic that comes out of such a mad mouth: it is the mouth of a horde, the mouth of a factory, the mouth of a station, the mouth of a slum.

"Snow is measured not by minutes but by winters. Seasons have no mechanical measure, their number is more like music. Drifting fog sings on over the cities and mercifully closes their eyes with no more new year and no more dateline.

"A new time has come. Atlas watches in his sleep."

But John is speaking in a foreign accent. How unfortunate!

XIII

After this calculated attack upon his philosophy everyone eagerly looks to see how Martin will stand up and for the first time move the world with his anger. But instead he only argues with himself. He cannot get clear of his own scruples, and though he brags, he instantly calls himself a liar almost in the same breath as he accuses John of the most shameful infamies. Martin, then, in attacking John, Eva, and even you, dear reader, ends by moving no one but himself. But here is what he says:

"This is a new game with new rules and I'm the one who plays the whole game and makes all the rules. That's why I regard myself as global imperative number one and I stand ready with new corporate enterprise without additional proof that the product is either needed or desired. Skilled propagandists try to make you less willing to spend and I hear them all around us now walking up and down inside the last wall that is left standing. I warn you these agents are undermining the long-term dependability of my Hi-line global operation for service to friendly outlanders and even to natives. Who would refuse an instant connection with my staff of entertainment Kings and world famous playmates? Yet I am betrayed by indeterminate boyish looking agents gnawing toward me under the oilcloth and if they don't stop I'LL FIRE!"

"Jump, you fool," cries John, scarcely hiding his merriment; but Martin replies that he cannot jump, "because," he says, "my foot's caught."

In this strange manner the whole human race comes to an end, and all because of our infatuation with numbers!

The Early Legend

NOTES FOR A COSMIC MEDITATION

"God alone is worthy of supreme seriousness. But man is made God's plaything and that is the best part of him. Therefore every man and woman should live life accordingly, and play the noblest games and be of another mind from what they are at present. . . . For they deem war a serious thing, though in war there is neither play nor culture worthy the name, which are the things *we* deem most serious. Hence all must live at peace as well as they possibly can. What, then, is the right way of living? Life must be lived as play, . . . then a man will be able to propitiate the gods and defend himself against his enemies."

Plato, *Laws*, VII, 803.

I

TAKE thought, man, tonight. Take thought, man, tonight when it is dark, when it is raining. Take thought of the game you have forgotten. You are the child of a great and peaceful race. You are the son of an unutterable fable. You were discovered on a mild mountain. You have come up out of the godlike ocean. You are holy, disarmed, signed with a chaste emblem. You are also marked with forgetfulness. Deep inside your breast you wear the number of loss. Take thought, man, to-

125

night. Do this. Do this. Recover your original name.
This is the early legend that returns. This is the legend
that begins again. Remember the ancient dances.
(He has remembered the whole world at peace. He
has remembered the world of villages, of maize, of
emeralds, of quiet mothers.
He has lifted up the world.)

(*They bring out drums and arrange them on the sand.
They begin to beat the drums. Three on one side, three
on the other. They beat their drums by the ocean.*)

Take time to compose yourself.
(The deep air of the lifting night!)
Do this, do this, friend, while drums call to mind the
deep night. Lift up your heart! (My heart swims in the
new tent which is immense night!)
Now the mind's eye burns like sun in the chaos of forgetfulness. Whose great strength comes up out of the
dark, sweeter than this small sun? Breathe in, friend.
Breathe in, friend. Inhale the sweetness of Africa. You
are the son of an unspeakable father.

Contemplation of water under the thunder, of fire under
the water, of air under the ocean, where time is born,
the roots of the sea. He watches the sunken ship. The
night is older.
He has lifted up the night.

126

He has lifted up the ocean. (He will lift up the shaggy hull to the dripping sun!) It is his heart, at the bottom of the sea, that moves the waves of the thunder.

II

MY birthday was in March, when the weather was furious. I was born in a scholar's town, a small town of famous men. The sign of the Ram. A choleric sign, it promised energy. I do not pretend to excuse all my actions: but from the first, I was a very merry, strong child.

My place of birth was a rich establishment called the "Hotel Everywhere."

Oh I remember well the golden hours of time all around me in the water, when I was still young! And I said to my mother: "Time is very warm!" "You must learn," said a certain mythical preceptor who had been assigned to me, "to run very far without tiring and to tell the truth." He had been the teacher of many heroes, whom I aspired to equal.
We sang music together by the river, I and my sisters, who were known later as nine mountains.

I became an unbloody priest. My hands and my hair turned into corn. I was given power to reconcile the earth with the seasons. I died repeatedly.

127

I died in the strong light of the sun, of thirst; the rocks all around me were crying out for summer. It was lovely to be twenty-one that morning! The whole world echoed to the dancing of my drum.

III

But did you ever know the whole world was once held prisoner in a bank?

Yes, it was on Cotton Street, and was called the Lotus Bank.
All the gold-barred windows used to jig with small-town tunes. (These were the inmates' beau ideal.)
As to the police world, it wore a cowboy hat (to hide the bald head of finance and thoughts of impotence, together with the velleities of clever mechanical war). The inmates were all white-haired juveniles with smooth repugnant chins; weak-eyed economic wizards whom I refused to acknowledge as friends.

I made myself a black man so as not to be one of them.

They shined solemnly, they crowed at me, they spouted water, they roused up their dogs. They were glorious in their cells until the land rang with statements. But I had made myself black so as not to be one of them.

Now you will find the Lotus Bank on Cotton Street where happiness is on sale for the best of them only and the joy belongs to some. And you will find the Harmony Bank on Grunt Street where the drinks are liberal for a few and fortune rains full force on the shanks of the many. And you will find another bank on Riley Street, where the police dogs bury their bones and live the life appropriate to their address.

Each prison is built like a Corinthian temple. Each is solemn like the ghats. Each is pretty as the morning sun. And you will see the Magnolia Bank on Water Street to which the whole world turns for simple sustenance: it is built like the Temple of Victory, but the halls are without worship and without faith, only the sign says "Happiness for some." And the happiness sings a small-town tune of the old times not too long ago to be forgotten.

But I made myself into a black man so as not to join in their song.

It is morning. Smoke goes up from the ghats. Sprinkle the oily river, friend, with the ashes of the satisfied.

Brahmins in cowboy hats,
strumming on the old banjo,
light their cigars at the ghats

where happy Brahmins go.
These are the ashes of a civilization.
Or don't you know?

I turned myself into a man of Africa, so as not to mingle with their ashes.

(Come on kid you may be right this could be a crematory like you suggest but there just isn't anything that can't be glamorized bring them all down to the ghats in bathing suits there's always a new thrill why be a damn pessimist you may be all right in your way but those people are basically different sure you can tell by the smoke what is going on but it can be glamorized there's nothing around here that can't be fixed up by a sweet chick in a bikini.)

Well, I said nothing. I went to work on my drum.

IV

With great speed I set the young man free. He sat up and spoke. The flowers were glad. Then there were people on the sand, and ships coming over the ocean: for by now, my country lay over the ocean.

How they smiled! We have found, we have found the places where the rain is deep and silent. We have found the fountains of the spring, where the Lord emerges refreshed every morning! He has laid His hand upon our shoulders, and our heart, like a bird, has spoken!

His words were wild wrens, and had words rolling in their throats: for He who sang in their bodies was the center of planets!

His thoughts were quails on the palace wall at Knossos,
quails in the mountains behind Phaestos,
which know him today, for the birds have not changed.

We have found the places where the Lord of Songs,
where the Nameless lies down in groves
making his light too shy. The valley flowers
with him. He sleeps in the sacred meadow;
he wakes in rain on the secular hill.
We have found him to be neither one nor the other,
neither sacred nor secular.

The quails whistling in the meadow
are the same as those on the palace wall.
The painted quail is sacred.
The live quail is neither sacred nor secular.

We have found places where the Lord of Songs
visits his beloved. Crossroads. Hilltops. Market towns.
Ball courts. Harbors. Crossroads. Meeting places.
Bridges. Places where the Lord of Songs
is refreshed. Crossroads.
It is when the Stranger is met and known
at the unplanned crossing
that the Nameless becomes a Name.

The silent plain. The bell in the morning.
The place where bread is broken,
where the host sees the pilgrim
and Man acquires a Name.
The Lord of Songs is always the familiar person,
neither sacred nor secular.

They came from the hill: Cretans, Minoans, Mayas,
        Incas,
to the crossing of the dusty stone god.
A little sweet smoke. Crickets in the field. They came
        from the hill city.
The smell of bread. The smell of maize. The Lord of
        the Songs
sought his beloved in the cornfield.
(The dusty stone is sacred.
The live maize is neither sacred nor secular.)
All the silent races came down from the hills
to the crossroads.

132

I went to them, I embraced my brothers whom I had now seen for the first time. They laid upon my shoulders hands without weapons and we saw one another in the eyes.

The plain where we met was high, among mountains: and there was a ceremonial ball game, with music, such as we played ten thousand years ago on our own mountain (yes, this was our mountain!).

It was a game with four goals on the four sides of the field: and the ball was supposed to be the universe, and the name of the game was: Here is God Who plays among His own children!

V

When night falls
beat one drum
in honor of night.

Maxims of the High Priest:
out of fire
the Bronze Word
"weapon."

The stranger
is holy.
With a consecrated blade
question his fountain
of sacred life.

Maxims of the High Priest:
strangers as sacrifice,
sacrum facere,
twice sacred.

Out of the fire
the iron question.
"Learn his source."

When night falls
beat one drum
in honor of night.

The High Priest
learns his maxims
in a secret dialogue
with fire.

Words of the forge:
discover
the stranger's origin;
you may find
his fountain.

134

Maxim:
try it again
with a double axe.

When night falls
beat one drum
in honor of night.

VI

OUT of the rain and the darkness and the depths, the
bottomless holes in the green sea, the shadows of a religious chaos, come fires holy and primitive, fires without voice, fires of glory, of fury; sudden and lingering
fires, coming and going; hasty fires, fires printed on the
horizon, starting and staying, removing, lost, forgotten,
remembered, parting and ascending, vanishing over the
water, emerging, and departing fires.

There is no voice with which to name these lightnings,
there is no eye to apprehend them, there is no thought
traveling over the water to the horizon, there is nothing
in the air but rain. There is no fear in the rain, there is
no hesitation on the sea. There is only one fire all over
the sea running about in rain upon the surface of the
new world . . . and departing.

There is no way to compute the age of these unbounded fires; there is no surmising the extent of their wandering courses, or to find the origin of the waters either, the young waters, fresh and salt seas, thrashing together, shivering at times with blue and green ardors. None of this is heard. Nothing has been recorded. All has vanished. All has reappeared.

The flames sometimes have color without force. At other times heat without light, burning fiercely. Sometimes they are only seen and not heard, sometimes felt and feared at a great distance, sometimes they come across the waters like brass horses. Sometimes their heat is felt only in the iron caverns of the heart.

Out of the tornadoes and the shadow of the south, out of the heat of the equator into which the lightning has departed, out of the sea exploding on the western shore, naked fishermen leap from their boats into the surf, to come out covered with water and with pride. Trees are bent double at the constant murmur of fear and of contentment passing always like a flying bird's shadow across the countenances of the grass houses. These men have gone into the darkness and the familiarity of their houses and the world is now empty.

Out of the tornadoes of the equator come secret fires raging upon the calm waters of the Pacific.

The spirits have held out toward us in their hands in silence, and in their hands their orchids and oranges. They have mocked us and made a fable of our passing by; they have sung to us, they have followed us, friendly. They have left us, and returned to ensnare us again; they have surrounded us; they have kissed our feet; they have vanished. They have mutinied; they have repented, stolen up to us with prayers; they have licked our hands; they have laughed and rolled at our feet; they have fawned upon us like beasts; they have enticed us; they have flown seductively about our heads; they have vanished into the sky. We have not understood their playful modes. We have fought Eros.

They have ruined us with their fists and suddenly turned pale and friendly and have sung to us ancient songs of our own land mingled with foreign music. They have come boiling out of the earth to leave emeralds and gold mixed in the cooling lava. No one has seen the streams of clear water containing these emeralds. They roll in the bottom of the rivers and no one finds them. The fires are those of the land promised to my father and mother. And to their fathers and their mothers. The fires are those of the land shown to me in sleep. The fires are those of a new world that has not been discovered and of an old world that has never been known. I do not recognize the names of the men who come up out of those fires with diamonds in their hands, but I look up out of the sea and count the incredible mountains: Volcán Cayambe, Volcán Cotopaxi, Volcán Coliachi, Volcán Sangay . . . and after that the jungle.

Readings from Ibn Abbad

NOTE: Ibn Abbad of Ronda was a Moslem, born in the citadel of Ronda, Andalusia, in 1332. In his youth he left Spain to study at Fez in Morocco, a most important religious center for medieval Islam. He never returned to Spain. He devoted himself to the study of law and of the Koran, but finding that law was "trifling" and looking for the deeper meaning of the Koran he joined a community of Sufis at Salé. Having attained to mystical illumination (at Tangier, 1363?), he returned to Fez to guide and instruct others. About 1380 he was appointed Imam and preacher at the main mosque of the Holy City of Fez and exercised a powerful spiritual influence until his death in 1390 (3 Ragab, 792, A.H.). He is of special interest to students of Western mysticism because some scholars believe that he exercised at least an indirect influence on the Spanish mystic, St. John of the Cross. Like St. John of the Cross, Doctor of the "Dark Night of the Soul," Ibn Abbad taught that it is in the night of desolation that the door to mystical union is secretly opened, though it remains tightly closed during the "day" of understanding and light. There is a resemblance between the two teachings, but scholars today do not agree there is clear proof of any influence.

The "readings" which follow are simply meditative and poetic notations made on texts of Ibn Abbad, given in French translation in the recent study by Father Paul Nwyia, S.J., *Ibn Abbad de Ronda*, Beyrouth, 1961. The purpose of these notes is to share something of an encounter with a rich and fervent religious personality of Islam, in whom the zeal of the Sufis is revealed, in an interesting way, against the cultural background of medieval Morocco. There is a mordant, realistic and human quality in the life and doctrine of this contemplative.

1 : *Ibn Abbad Described by a Friend* (Ibn Qunfud)

Among those I met at Fez, let me mention the celebrated
preacher

The Holy Man Abu Abdallah Mahammad ben Ibrahim
ben Abbad ar Rundi

Whose father was an eloquent and distinguished
preacher.

Abu Abdallah is a sage,

A recollected man in whom renunciation and great kind-
ness are one . . .

He speaks admirably of *Tasawwuf*.[1]

His writings are worthy to be read to the brothers as
they practice *Dikr*.[2]

He never returns the visits of the Sultan

But he assists at spiritual concerts (*sama*) on the night
of *Mawlid*.[3]

I have never found him sitting with anyone in a social
gathering.

Whoever would see Abu Abdallah Mahammad must
seek him out in his own cell.

At times I begged his prayers. This only made him
blush with confusion.

---

[1] *Tasawwuf*—Sufism: the way of poverty and mystic enlighten-
ment.

[2] *Dikr*—systematic method of prayer and concentration in which
breathing techniques are united with rhythmic invocation of Allah.

[3] Feast of the nativity of the Prophet Mohammed.

Of all the pleasures of this world he permits himself
    none
Save only perfumes and incense
Which he uses lavishly:
Indeed, the Sultan tried to equal him in this
But failed.
And Abu Abdallah Mahammad has taught
That the Holy Prophet himself
Used incense copiously to prepare for his encounters
    with angels.
He takes care of his own household affairs
And has never taken a wife or a mistress
For above all things he prizes peace
And tranquillity of soul.
At home he wears patched garments
And, when he goes outdoors,
A white or a green mantle.

2: *The Burial Place of Ibn Abbad*

He was buried in a vacant property, for he was a
    stranger
And had not built himself a tomb in that city, or in any
    other.
After a few years the wall of the lot fell down
But later, the City Governor
Built the saint a small dome,

Confiding to his secretary the care
To take up the offerings left there
And send them to the saint's family.

Meanwhile the Guild of Shoemakers
Took him as patron. Each year
On the evening of his death in Ragab[4]
They come in procession for a vigil there
With lights, readings and songs,
For in his lifetime
The saint was their friend.
He sat in their shops, conversed with them.
He prayed for the apprentices
To save them from piercing awls
And giant needles.
Often in the Mosque
He led the shoemakers in prayer.
Today, however, he is forgotten.

3: *Prayer and Sermon of Ibn Abbad*

O Mighty One:
Let me not constrain
Thy servants!

4 *Ragab*—June.

I44

O men:
Your days are not without change and number.
Life passes more quickly than a train of camels.
Old age is the signal
To take the road.
It is death that is truth,
Not life, the impossible!
Why then do we turn away from truth?
The way is plain!

O men:
This life
Is only a blinking eye.

O men:
The last end of all our desire:
May He draw close to us
The Living, the Unchanging.
May He move toward us
His huge Majesty
(If it be possible to bear it!)
His Glory!

O men:
Burn away impure desire
In His Glory!

4: *Desolation*

For the servant of God
Consolation is the place of danger
Where he may be deluded
(Accepting only what he sees,
Experiences, or knows)
But desolation is his home:
For in desolation he is seized by God
And entirely taken over into God,
In darkness, in emptiness,
In loss, in death of self.
Then the self is only ashes. Not even ashes!

5: *To Belong to Allah*

To belong to Allah
Is to see in your own existence
And in all that pertains to it
Something that is neither yours
Nor from yourself,
Something you have on loan;
To see your being in His Being,
Your subsistence in His Subsistence,
Your strength in His Strength:
Thus you will recognize in yourself
His title to possession of you

As Lord,
And your own title as servant:
Which is Nothingness.

6: *Letter to a Sufi Who Has Abandoned Sufism to
    Study Law*

Well, my friend, you prefer jurisprudence to contem-
    plation!
If you intend to spend your time collecting authorities
    and precedents
What advice do you want from me?
I can tell you this: each man, today,
Gets what he wants,
Except that no one has discovered a really perfect
Way to kill time.
Those who do not have to work for a living
Are engrossed in every kind of nonsense,
And those who must gain their livelihood
Are so absorbed in this that they
Have time for nothing else.
As to finding someone capable of spiritual life
Ready to do work that is clean of passion
And inordinate desire
Done only for love of Allah—
This is a way of life in which no one is interested
Except a few who have received the special
Mercy of Allah.

Are you aware of this? Are you sure of your condition?
Well then, go ahead with your books of Law,
It will make little difference whether you do this
Or something else equally trivial.
You will gain nothing by it, and perhaps lose nothing:
You will have found a way to kill time.
As you say: you prefer to spend your time doing things
        you are used to.
Drunkards and lechers would agree:
They follow the same principle.

7: *To a Novice*

Avoid three kinds of Master:
Those who esteem only themselves,
For their self-esteem is blindness;
Those who esteem only innovations,
For their opinions are aimless,
Without meaning;
Those who esteem only what is established;
Their minds
Are little cells of ice.

All these three
Darken your inner light
With complicated arguments
And hatred of Sufism.

He who finds Allah
Can lack nothing.
He who loses Allah
Can possess nothing.

He who seeks Allah will be made clean in tribulation,
His heart will be more pure,
His conscience more sensitive in tribulation
Than in prayer and fasting.
Prayer and fasting may perhaps
Be nothing but self-love, self-gratification,
The expression of hidden sin
Ruining the value of these works.
But tribulation
Strikes at the root!

8: *To a Novice*

Be a son of this instant:
It is a messenger of Allah
And the best of messengers
Is one who announces your indigence,
Your nothingness.
Be a son of this instant,
Thanking Allah
For a mouthful of ashes.

9: *To a Novice*

The fool is one
Who strives to procure at each instant
Some result
That Allah has not willed.

10: *Letter to One Who Has Abandoned The Way*

Our friend X brought me your letter—*one* letter—informing me of your present state. One letter, not two or three as you contend. And thank God for it, since if there had been two or three I would have had to answer them all and I have no taste for that.

Since you have left me, your conduct is an uninterrupted betrayal of Allah, the Prophet, the Law and the Way of Sufism. And yet Allah had ennobled you in the state of poverty, and had bound you more tightly than others to religion and *Tasawwuf,* so that your admiration of the friends of God had become your life's breath. Thus you were obligated to remain faithful and preserve this vocation from all that might corrupt it!

Yet you did nothing of the kind. You have taken the exact opposite path. You have made all reconciliation impossible. And worse: you have cast off religion entirely to run after trifles that even fools would despise, let alone men of reason.

And on top of all that you have betrayed me for an onion, for a turd, rather, since an onion can have some use!

Yet in spite of all this, there is the will of Allah which I do not measure; there is the power of Allah to which no limit can be imposed; and if Allah wishes to give the lie to my doubts of your possible conversion, that is not hard for Him to do.

As for me, I can help only by prayer.

But what help is that, if you do not help me by a sincere return?

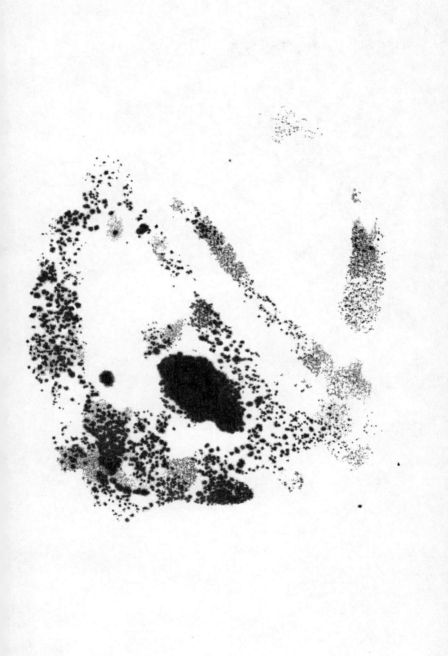

Message to Poets

NOTE: This message was read at a meeting of the "new" Latin-American poets—and a few young North Americans—Mexico City, February 1964. This was not a highly organized and well-financed international congress, but a spontaneous and inspired meeting of young poets from all over the hemisphere, most of whom could barely afford to be there. One, for instance, sold her piano to make the trip from Peru.

WE who are poets know that the reason for a poem is not discovered until the poem itself exists. The reason for a living act is realized only in the act itself. This meeting is a spontaneous explosion of hopes. That is why it is a venture in prophetic poverty, supported and financed by no foundation, organized and publicized by no official group, but a living expression of the belief that there are now in our world new people, new poets who are not in tutelage to established political systems or cultural structures—whether communist or capitalist —but who dare to hope in their own vision of reality and of the future. This meeting is united in a flame of hope whose temperature has not yet been taken and whose effects have not yet been estimated, because it is a new fire. The reason for the fire cannot be apparent to one who is not warmed by it. The reason for being here will not be found until all have walked together, without afterthought, into contradictions and possibilities.

We believe that our future will be made by love and hope, not by violence or calculation. The Spirit of Life that has brought us together, whether in space or only in agreement, will make our encounter an epiphany of certainties we could not know in isolation.

The solidarity of poets is not planned and welded together with tactical convictions or matters of policy, since these are affairs of prejudice, cunning, and design. Whatever his failures, the poet is not a cunning man. His art depends on an ingrained innocence which he would lose in business, in politics, or in too organized a form of academic life. The hope that rests on calculation has lost its innocence. We are banding together to defend our innocence.

All innocence is a matter of belief. I do not speak now of organized agreement, but of interior personal convictions "in the spirit." These convictions are as strong and undeniable as life itself. They are rooted in fidelity to *life* rather than to artificial systems. The solidarity of poets is an elemental fact like sunlight, like the seasons, like the rain. It is something that cannot be organized, it can only happen. It can only be "received."

156

It is a gift to which we must remain open. No man can plan to make the sun rise or the rain fall. The sea is still wet in spite of all formal and abstract programs. Solidarity is not collectivity. The organizers of collective life will deride the seriousness or the reality of our hope. If they infect us with their doubt we shall lose our innocence and our solidarity along with it.

Collective life is often organized on the basis of cunning, doubt and guilt. True solidarity is destroyed by the political art of pitting one man against another and the commercial art of estimating all men at a price. On these illusory measurements men build a world of arbitrary values without life and meaning, full of sterile agitation. To set one man against another, one life against another, one work against another, and to express the measurement in terms of cost or of economic privilege and moral honor is to infect everybody with the deepest metaphysical doubt. Divided and set up against one another for the purpose of evaluation, men immediately acquire the mentality of objects for sale in a slave market. They despair of themselves because they know they have been unfaithful to life and to being, and they no longer find anyone to forgive the infidelity.

Yet their despair condemns them to further infidelity: alienated from their own spiritual roots, they contrive to break, to humiliate and to destroy the spirit of others. In such a situation there is no joy, only rage. Each man

157

feels the deepest root of his being poisoned by suspicion, unbelief and hate. Each man experiences his very existence as guilt and betrayal, and as a possibility of death: nothing more.

We stand together to denounce the shame and the imposture of all such calculations.

✳ If we are to remain united against these falsehoods, against all power that poisons man, and subjects him to the mystifications of bureaucracy, commerce and the police state, we must refuse the price tag. We must refuse academic classification. We must reject the seductions of publicity. We must not allow ourselves to be pitted one against another in mystical comparisons—political, literary or cultural orthodoxies. We must not be made to devour and dismember one another for the amusement of their press. We must not let ourselves be eaten by them to assuage their own insatiable doubt. We must not merely be *for* something and *against* something else, even if we are for "ourselves" and against "them." Who are "they"? Let us not give them support by becoming an "opposition" which assumes they are definitively real.

Let us remain outside "their" categories. It is in this sense that we are all monks: for we remain innocent and invisible to publicists and bureaucrats. They cannot imagine what we are doing unless we betray ourselves to them, and even then they will never be able.

158

They understand nothing except what they themselves have decreed. They are crafty ones who weave words about life and then make life conform to what they themselves have declared. How can they trust anyone when they make life itself tell lies? It is the businessman, the propagandist, the politician, not the poet, who devoutly believes in "the magic of words."

For the poet there is precisely no magic. There is only life in all its unpredictability and all its freedom. All magic is a ruthless venture in manipulation, a vicious circle, a self-fulfilling prophecy.

Word-magic is an impurity of language and of spirit in which words, deliberately reduced to unintelligibility, appeal mindlessly to the vulnerable will. Let us deride and parody this magic with other variants of the unintelligible, if we want to. But it is better to prophesy than to deride. To prophesy is not to predict, but to seize upon reality in its moment of highest expectation and tension toward the new. This tension is discovered not in hypnotic elation but in the light of everyday existence. Poetry is innocent of prediction because it is itself the fulfillment of all the momentous predictions hidden in everyday life.

Poetry is the flowering of ordinary possibilities. It is the fruit of ordinary and natural choice. This is its innocence and dignity.

Let us not be like those who wish to make the tree

bear its fruit first and the flower afterwards—a conjuring trick and an advertisement. We are content if the flower comes first and the fruit afterwards, in due time. Such is the poetic spirit.

Let us obey life, and the Spirit of Life that calls us to be poets, and we shall harvest many new fruits for which the world hungers—fruits of hope that have never been seen before. With these fruits we shall calm the resentments and the rage of man.

Let us be proud that we are not witch doctors, only ordinary men.

Let us be proud that we are not experts in anything. Let us be proud of the words that are given to us for nothing; not to teach anyone, not to confute anyone, not to prove anyone absurd, but to point beyond all objects into the silence where nothing can be said.

We are not persuaders. We are the children of the Unknown. We are the ministers of silence that is needed to cure all victims of absurdity who lie dying of a contrived joy. Let us then recognize ourselves for who we are: dervishes mad with secret therapeutic love which cannot be bought or sold, and which the politician fears more than violent revolution, for violence changes nothing. But love changes everything.

We are stronger than the bomb.

Let us then say "yes" to our own nobility by embracing the insecurity and abjection that a dervish existence entails.

160

In the Republic of Plato there was already no place for poets and musicians, still less for dervishes and monks. As for the technological Platos who think they now run the world we live in, they imagine they can tempt us with banalities and abstractions. But we can elude them merely by stepping into the Heraklitean river which is never crossed twice.

When the poet puts his foot in that ever-moving river, poetry itself is born out of the flashing water. In that unique instant, the truth is manifest to all who are able to receive it.

No one can come near the river unless he walks on his own feet. He cannot come there carried in a vehicle.

No one can enter the river wearing the garments of public and collective ideas. He must feel the water on his skin. He must know that immediacy is for naked minds only, and for the innocent.

Come, dervishes: here is the water of life. Dance in it.

Answers on Art and Freedom

NOTE: These lines were written in reply to nine questions asked by readers of the magazine *Eco Contemporaneo,* Buenos Aires, and were reprinted in the *Lugano Review.* I no longer have the questions, but they may be guessed. They were simple enough, and were all concerned with the familiar topic of the artist's autonomy in his own sphere. The artist is responsible first of all for the excellence of his *work* and his art should not be used for an ulterior purpose that conflicts with this primary aim. All this is obvious enough in theory. Not being perfectly informed, I do not know how far, in practice, the artist is perversely "used" or controlled by society. I assume that the questions were formulated chiefly with a mind to protest against all forms of official—especially political—censorship. Taking for granted that political oppression is obnoxious, these answers seek deeper motives and principles of freedom within the artist himself, and they concern themselves chiefly with the artist in Western society.

I AM asked whether or not the artist, writer, poet, is a docile servant of institutions, or whether he can and should work in complete freedom. Stated in these terms the proposition would seem to be deceptively simple.

One would mechanically answer that the artist is by his very nature free and autonomous. He can be nobody's slave. There is no problem. Everyone sees the answer. It is even *to the interest of those who control him* to allow the artist his autonomy. The relative freedom that is suddenly granted to a Soviet poet becomes a matter of great importance to the whole world. It tends to make people think more kindly and more hopefully of Soviet Russia. Whereas the poet who rebels completely against conventional Western society (Rimbaud, Baudelaire, the Beats) establishes that society more firmly in its complacent philistinism, he also strengthens its conviction that all artists are by necessity opium fiends and feeds its sense of magnanimity in tolerating such people.

What I mean to say by this is that the enemies of the artist's freedom are those who most profit by his *seeming* to be free, whether or not he is so.

And the artist himself, to the extent that he is dominated by introjected philistine condemnations of his art, pours out his energy and integrity in resisting these tyrannical pressures which come to him from within himself. His art then wastes itself in reaction against the anti-art of the society in which he lives (or he cultivates anti-art as a protest against the art cult of the society in which he lives).

The artist who expends all his efforts in convincing himself that he is not a non-artist or the anti-artist who struggles not to become "an artist," cannot justify his

166

vexations by appealing to an ideal of freedom. What he needs is not an ideal of freedom, but at least a minimum of practical and subjective autonomy—freedom from the internalized emotional pressures by which society holds him down. I mean freedom of conscience. This is a spiritual value and its roots are ultimately religious. Hence my first principle is that since in our society everybody is already more or less concerned with a theoretical and doctrinaire approach to the question of art and freedom, maybe the artist himself has something better to do—namely his own job. There have grown up so many myths about the business of "being an artist" and living the special kind of life that artists are reputed to live, that if the artist is too concerned with "being an artist" he will never get around to doing any work. Hence it is to his advantage, first of all, to be free from myths about "Art" and even from myths about the threat which society offers to his "freedom." This applies, at least, to artists living in "the West" where in fact nobody is seriously interfering with his freedom. On the other hand, under Communism the poets and painters seem to be the most serious prophets of a genuine liberation for thought, life and experience. They protest more articulately than anyone against the general servility to boredom and official stupidity.

Yet the artist who is held by dope or drink is just as much a prisoner of a corrupt commercial or political power structure as the artist who is held by the coercion of the Writer's Union. Each in his own way is turning out propaganda by producing something according to the dictates of the society in which he lives. The artist who is really free and chooses this particular servitude is perhaps less worthy of admiration than one who, being subject to all kinds of harassment, still makes the choice for which Sartre praised the men of the French resistance under Nazism.

1 : What is the *use* of art? The artist must serenely defend his right to be completely useless. It is better to produce absolutely no work of art at all than to do what can be cynically "used." Yet anything can be used—even the most truculently abstract paintings. They decorate the offices of corporation presidents who have quickly caught on to the fact that to pay ten thousand dollars for something explicitly "useless" is a demonstration of one's wealth and power—as well as of sophistication.

And tomorrow the abstract paintings will be on the walls of the Commissars.

Works of art can be and are used in many ways but such uses are beyond the range of this question. "Art" considered as an immanent perfection of the artist's own intelligence is not improved by non-artistic use. Let us set aside the question of a supposed cult of pure art, art for art's sake, etc. Is this an actual problem? I doubt it. Who is to say what poets and artists as a species are thinking and doing? The world is full of poets, novelists, painters, sculptors: they blossom on all the bushes. Who can generalize about them, except perhaps to say that they all tend to start out looking for something that can't be found merely by selling insurance or automobiles.

The problem arises when art ceases to be honest work and becomes instead a way to self-advertisement and success—when the writer or painter uses his art merely to sell himself. (It is an article of faith, in Western society at least, that a poet or painter is by nature "more interesting" than other people and, God knows, everybody wants in the worst way to be interesting!)

2: The artist cannot afford passively to accept, to "reflect" or to celebrate what everybody likes. The artist who subscribes to the commercial slogan that the customer is always right will soon be deserted by everybody. The customer has now been trained to think that the *artist* is always right. Thus we have a new situation in which the artist feels himself obligated to function as a prophet or a magician. He sees that he has to be disconcerting, even offensive. Who will ever read him or buy him unless he occasionally insults the customer and all he believes in? That is precisely what the customer wants. He has delegated to the artist the task of nonconforming on his behalf—the task of not conforming with "ordinary decent people." Where does the artist go from there? In desperation he paints a meticulously accurate portrait of a beer can.

3: The writer who submits to becoming "an engineer of the soul" is in complicity with the secret police —or with the advertising business. He is worse than the policeman who does an honest job of work beating up his prisoner and extracting a confession. The "engineer of the soul" simply dictates routine and trivial testimonials to the rightness of an absurd society without any cost to himself and without need to make use of art in any form whatever. For this he receives certain rewards with which he is content.

4: *The artist in uniform.* Precisely when does it cease to be respectable to be seen marching with the political police? It is a nice question in countries where, rightly or wrongly, one is considered to be alive only if he is agitating for revolution. Putting the question in another form: how do you know when *your* revolution has developed sclerosis?

5: *Art and ethics.* Certainly the artist has no obligation to promulgate ethical lessons any more than political or economic ones. The artist is not a catechist. Usually moral directives are lost when one attempts to convey them in a medium that is not intended to communicate conceptual formulas. But the artist has a moral obligation to maintain his own freedom and his own truth. His art and his life are separable only in theory. The artist cannot be free in his art if he does not have a conscience that warns him when he is acting like a slave in his everyday life.

The artist should preach nothing—not even his own autonomy. His art should speak its own truth, and in so doing it will be in harmony with every other kind of truth—moral, metaphysical, and mystical.

The artist has no moral obligation to prove himself one of the elect by systematically standing a traditional moral code on its head.

6: Is the artist necessarily committed to this or that political ideology? No. but he does live in a world where politics are decisive and where political power can destroy his art as well as his life. Hence he is indirectly committed to seek some political solution to problems that endanger the freedom of man. This is the great temptation: there is not a single form of government or social system today that does not in the end seek to manipulate or to coerce the artist in one way or another. In every case the artist should be in complete solidarity with those who are fighting for rights and freedom against inertia, hypocrisy and coercion: e.g. the Negroes in the United States.

The American Negroes are at once the ones who fight for their freedom and who exemplify a genuine and living creativity, for example in jazz.

7: "Formalism"—a meaningless cliché devised by literary and artistic gendarmes. It is a term totally devoid of value or significance, as are all the other cultural slogans invented in the police station.

8: I do not consider myself integrated in the war-making society in which I live, but the problem is that this society *does* consider *me* integrated in it. I notice that for nearly twenty years my society—or those in it who read my books—have decided upon an identity for me and insist that I continue to correspond perfectly to the idea of me which they found upon reading my first successful book. Yet the same people simultaneously prescribe for me a contrary identity. They demand that I remain forever the superficially pious, rather rigid and somewhat narrow-minded young monk I was twenty years ago, and at the same time they continually circulate the rumor that I have left my monastery. What has actually happened is that I have been simply living where I am and developing in my own way without consulting the public about it since it is none of the public's business.

9: Society benefits when the artist liberates himself from its coercive or seductive pressures. Only when he is obligated to his fellow man in the concrete, rather than to society in the abstract can the artist have anything to say that will be of value to others. His art then becomes accidentally a work of love and justice. The artist would do well, however, not to concern himself too much with "society" in the abstract or with ideal "commitments." This has not always been true. It applies more to our time when "society" is in some confusion. It is conceivable that the artist might once again be completely integrated in society as he was in the Middle Ages. Today he is hardly likely to find himself unless he is a non-conformist and a rebel. To say this is neither dangerous nor new. It is what society really expects of its artists. For today the artist has, whether he likes it or not, inherited the combined functions of hermit, pilgrim, prophet, priest, shaman, sorcerer, soothsayer, alchemist and bonze. How could such a man be free? How can he really "find himself" if he plays a role that society has predetermined for him? The freedom of the artist is to be sought precisely in the choice of his *work* and not in the choice of the role as "artist" which society asks him to play, for reasons that will always remain very mysterious.

To conclude: the artist must not delude himself that he has an infinite capacity to choose for himself and a moral responsibility to exercise this unlimited choice, especially when it becomes absurd.

If he does this, then let him take my word for it, he will find himself with the same problem and in the same quandary as those monks who have vegetated for three centuries in a moral morass of abstract voluntarism. There is a great deal of ambiguity in the facile rationalization which says that even in the worst and most confined of situations you can become perfectly free simply by *choosing* the situation you are in. Freedom consists in something more than merely choosing what is forced upon you—and doing so with a certain exultation at the absurdity and the humiliation that are involved. It takes more than this kind of choice to make one "the incontestable author of an event or of an object" (Sartre). At the same time, I wonder if this *need to be an incontestable author* points to freedom at all. On the contrary, maybe it is one of the roots of unfreedom in the psychology of the modern artist. As long as I am obsessed with the need to get myself or my work recognized as "incontestable" and "authentic," I am still under servitude to the myths and anxieties of my society and unable to attain the complete freedom of the artist who chooses his work of art in its own terms and in his, not in those of the market, or of politics, or of philosophy, or of the myth of pure experience, absolute spontaneity, and all the rest.

The impiety of the Sartrian who chooses the ugly, the absurd and the obscene as an act of which he is the "incontestable author" rejoins the piety of the monastic novice who chooses the most arbitrary and most pointless acts of self-mortification in order to see himself as pleasing to God. In either case there is a naive and narcissistic emphasis on the pure voluntaristic choice for its own sake. The supposed purity of this voluntarism is not purity at all: it is merely abstract willfulness.

174

True artistic freedom can never be a matter of sheer willfulness, or arbitrary posturing. It is the outcome of authentic possibilities, understood and accepted in their own terms, not the refusal of the concrete in favor of the purely "interior." In the last analysis, the only valid witness to the artist's creative freedom is his work itself. The artist builds his own freedom and forms his own artistic conscience, by the work of his hands. Only when the work is finished can he tell whether or not it was done "freely."

Signatures: Notes on the Author's Drawings

NOTE: The drawings reproduced in this book were selected from a collection exhibited in various cities in the United States. These "Notes" accompanied the exhibition.

SINCE judgments are usually based on comparisons and since opportunities for comparison in the visual arts today are so many and often so irrelevant as to be overwhelming, the viewer is not invited to regard the abstract drawings presented here as "works of art."

Nor is he urged to seek in them traces of irony. Nor need he read into them a conscious polemic against art. These signs lay claim to little more than a sort of crude innocence. They desire nothing but their constitutional freedom from polemic, from apologetic, and from program.

If the viewer is not encouraged to judge these drawings in terms of familiar categories, he is also urged not to consider himself in any way, implicitly or otherwise, judged by them. For it must be admitted that the ambiguities of abstraction tend to set some people on edge, as though accusing them of not understanding something that is doubtless not intended to be understood. But by now everyone knows that it is unwise to ask what abstractions are "of." These are not "drawings of."

It would be better if these abstractions did not have titles. However, titles were provided out of the air. The viewer will hardly be aided by them, but he may imagine himself aided if he wishes. The most deliberate titles, those of the Genesis series, are at best afterthoughts. In any case, the viewer who wants titles can make up his own.

Once this is admitted, there should not be too much trouble for the observer who desires to be at peace with these rude signs, provided that he is himself a basically peaceable man and content to accept life as it is, tolerating its unexpected manifestations, and not interpreting everything unfamiliar as a personal threat.

These abstractions—one might almost call them *graffiti* rather than calligraphies—are simple signs and ciphers of energy, acts or movements intended to be propitious. Their "meaning" is not to be sought on the level of convention or of concept. These are not conventional signs as are words, numbers, hieroglyphs, or symbols. They could not be assigned a reference by advance agreement because it has been their nature to appear on paper without previous agreement. On the contrary, the only "agreements" which they represent were momentary and unique, free, undetermined and inconclusive. They came to life when they did, in the form of reconciliations, as expressions of unique and unconscious harmonies appropriate to their own moment though not confined to it. But they do not register a past and personal experience, nor attempt to indicate playfully the passage of a special kind of artist, like footsteps in the snow. It is not important whether anyone passed here, because these signs are not sufficiently accounted for as records of "events." However, the seeing of them may open up a way to obscure reconciliations and agreements that are not arbitrary—or even to new, intimate histories.

In a world cluttered and programmed with an infinity of practical signs and consequential digits referring to business, law, government and war, one who makes such nondescript marks as these is conscious of a special vocation to be inconsequent, to be outside the sequence and to remain firmly alien to the program. In effect these writings are decidedly hopeful in their own way in so far as they stand outside all processes of production, marketing, consumption and destruction, which does not however mean that they cannot be bought. Nevertheless it is clear that these are not legal marks. Nor are they illegal marks, since as far as law is concerned they are perfectly inconsequent. It is this and this alone which gives them a Christian character (Galatians 5), since they obviously do not fit into any familiar setting of religious symbolism, liturgical or otherwise. But one must perhaps ask himself whether it has not now become timely for a Christian who makes a sign or a mark of some sort to feel free about it, and not consider himself rigidly predetermined to a system of glyphs that have a long cultural standing and are fully consequential, even to the point of seeming entirely relevant in the world of business, law, government and war.

Ciphers, signs without prearrangement, figures of reconciliation, notes of harmony, inventions perhaps, but not in the sense of "findings" arrived at by the contrived agreement of idea and execution. Summonses to awareness, but not to "awareness *of*." Neither rustic nor urbane, primitive nor modern, though they might suggest cave art, maybe Zen calligraphy. No need to categorize these marks. It is better if they remain unidentified vestiges, signatures of someone who is not around. If these drawings are able to persist in a certain autonomy and fidelity, they may continue to awaken possibilities, consonances; they may dimly help to alter one's perceptions. Or they may quietly and independently continue to invent themselves. Such is the "success" they aspire to. Doubtless there is more ambition than modesty in such an aim. For the only dream a man seriously has when he takes a brush in his hand and dips it into ink is to reveal a new sign that can continue to stand by itself and to exist in its own right, transcending all logical interpretation.